951
M   McLenighan, Valjean
        China
                              94-19

DATE DUE		
2 0 MAR 2 7 1995		
MAY 15 1996		

5-9

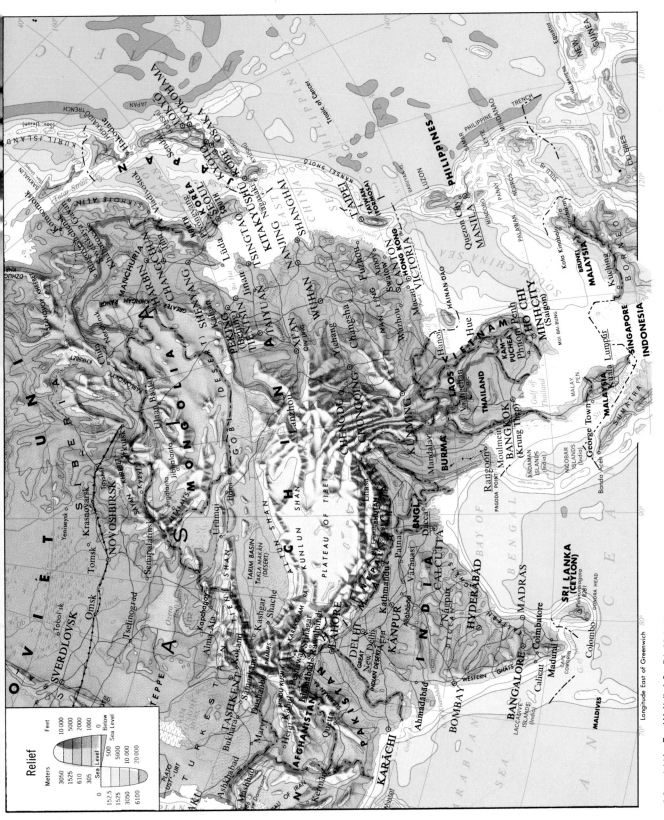

Relief

Meters	Feet
3050	10 000
1525	5000
610	2000
305	1000
0	Sea Level
Sea Level	0
	500
152.5	1525
1525	3050
3050	6100
6100	10 000
	20 000

Longitude East of Greenwich

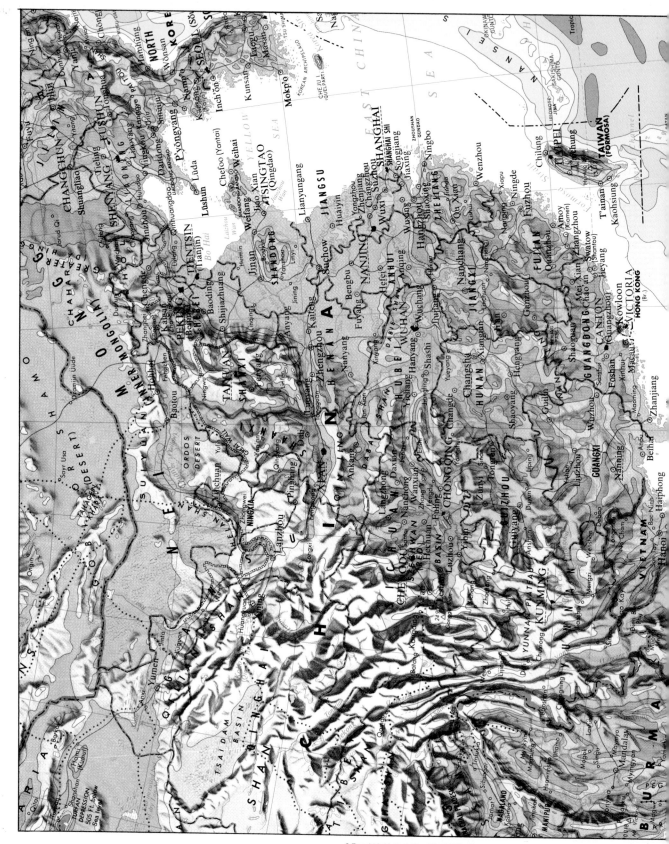

Enchantment of the World

CHINA

A History to 1949

By Valjean McLenighan

Consultants: Mikiso Hane, Ph.D., Szold Distinguished Service Professor of History, Knox College, Galesburg, Illinois

Stephen Burke, Undergraduate Asian Studies, University of Michigan, Ann Arbor

Consultant for Social Studies: Donald W. Nylin, Ph.D., Assistant Superintendent for Instruction, Aurora West Public Schools, Aurora, Illinois

Consultant for Reading: Robert L. Hillerich, Ph.D., Bowling Green State University, Bowling Green, Ohio.

 CHILDRENS PRESS, CHICAGO

Restoration of a King of Heaven (Protector of Buddha) in a Taoist Temple near Chang-chou

Library of Congress Cataloging in Publication Data

McLenighan, Valjean.
   China, a history to 1949.

   (Enchantment of the world)
   Includes index.
   Summary: Presents the history until 1949 of the
country with the oldest continuing history of any nation.
   1.   China—History—Juvenile literature.
[1.   China—History]   I.   Title.   II.   Series.
DS736.M38   1983   951   83-14260
ISBN 0-516-02754-9   AACR2

8 9 10 11 12 13 14 15 16 17 R 02 01 00 99 98 97 96 95 94 93

Picture Acknowledgments

Hillstrom Stock Photos— © Jack Lund: Cover, pages 46,
58, 74, 84, 109, 115, 123;
© Arthur Brown: Pages 4, 13, 17, 28, 37, 44, 48, 49, 55, 76
(top and bottom right), 82 (right), 96, 97, 122;
© Globe Photos: Page 5;
© Lawrence M. Nelson: Pages 11 (top), 16, 100;
© Andrew S. Burgess: Pages 50, 93

Picture Group— © John Hanlon: Pages 6, 8
Chandler Forman: Pages 11 (bottom), 77 (top left and
right), 82 (left)
Dr. Robert A. Clark/National Weather Service/NOAA:
Page 15
Metropolitan Museum of Art—Rogers Fund, 1943: Pages
19 (top), 27; Munsey Bequest, 1924: Page 22; Rogers Fund,
1932: Page 24; Rogers Fund, 1925: Page 25 (left); Gift of
Joseph J. Asch, 1936: Page 33; Gift of Mrs. Maurice
Casalis, 1945: Page 47; Rogers Fund, 1911: Page 54 (left);
Rogers Fund, 1922: Page 54 (right); Gift of the Dillon
Fund, 1973: Pages 60, 78; Gift of Mrs. Samuel T. Peters,
1926: Pages 65, 73; Gift of A.W. Bahr, 1947: Page 72; Gift
of Mr. and Mrs. Earl Morse, 1972: Page 79; Rogers Fund,
1918: Page 81; Gift of Heber R. Bishop, 1902: Page 87;
Bequest of Edward G. Kennedy, 1932: Page 88; Rogers
Fund, 1945: Page 94
**Ontario Science Centre, Toronto/China: 7000 Years of
Discovery:** Pages (19 bottom), 20, 25 (right), 41, 42, 45,
61, 62, 63, 67
Colour Library International: Pages 56, 110
Historical Pictures Service, Inc., Chicago: Pages 64, 71,
95, 98, 105, 108
Jerome Wyckoff: Pages 66, 76 (bottom left), 77 (bottom),
111
Len Meents: Maps on pages 12, 38, 52, 70, 80, 86, 107
**Courtesy Flag Research Center, Winchester,
Massachusetts 01890:** Flag on back cover
Cover: West Lake, Hangzhou

Near Lotus Peak on Jade Screen Mountain in the Huang Shan range

TABLE OF CONTENTS

The Great Wall of China was built in the third century B.C.

Chapter 1

THE CENTRAL KINGDOM

Imagine you're returning from your first trip into space. You are a few hundred miles above the earth, and the continent of Asia lies beneath you. For a long time you're lost in the beauty of the sight. The satellite photos you've seen are nothing compared with the real thing. Brilliant coastal blues and greens, snowcapped mountain peaks that shine like jewels in the crown of the continent—these hold you in their spell.

From 200 miles or so (about 300 kilometers) you can see the sandy sprawl of the great Gobi Desert, part of the boundary between the Soviet Union and China, the two largest countries in Asia. And then, as the earth looms closer, the Great Wall of China comes into view.

Snaking some 1,500 miles (2,400 kilometers) across the mountains and plains of northern China, the Great Wall is one of the wonders of the world. It is 30 feet (9 meters) high in places, and wide enough so that five horses abreast could thunder along it. Imagine trying to build such a wall today. The Great Wall was built in the third century B.C.! It took 300,000 workers nearly fourteen years to complete it.

The Great Wall is wide enough so that five horses abreast were able to thunder along it.

China's first emperor ordered the Great Wall into being. Earlier kings of small, independent states had begun to put up walls as far back as the fifth century B.C. to protect themselves from attacks by northern barbarians. Emperor Shih Huang-ti forged these smaller kingdoms into the Ch'in Empire in 221 B.C. By that time, a particularly fierce barbarian tribe, ancestors of the Huns, threatened to overrun the new empire. Shih Huang-ti joined the shorter walls into the Great Wall. From behind its battlements, the emperor waged war on the barbarians.

An eyewitness wrote of the barbarian wars: "The dead reached incalculable numbers; the corpses lay strewn for hundreds of miles, and streams of blood soaked the plains."

The question of what to do about the barbarians has been a major problem in China almost since the beginning, and it's still important today. During most of Chinese history, the word *barbarian* applied to anyone and everyone who was not Chinese— that is, to the entire rest of the world. Since ancient times the Chinese have been comfortable in the belief that China is superior to all other nations. They have thought of their country as the only real center of civilization, an island of culture in a sea of inferiors. In fact, the Chinese name for their kingdom, *Chung kuo,* means "Middle Kingdom" or "Central Kingdom."

In some cases the Chinese simply absorbed the barbarians into their way of life. In others, they fought bloody battles to repel invaders. But for the most part, as time went on, the Chinese way of dealing with the rest of the world was to let it go its own way. This method worked, on the whole, for just about two thousand years—right up until the nineteenth century.

By that time, however, the barbarians had become impossible to ignore. They had developed into great nations in their own right. While the Chinese had been content, by and large, to stay in their own part of the world, Europeans and then Americans had fought and traded their way into almost every corner of the globe. Their way of life depended on finding ever-expanding markets for trade. And they had the ships, soldiers, and weapons to impose their wishes on people who wanted nothing to do with them.

Within a few decades China was at the mercy of a group of barbarian nations that actually considered the Chinese inferior! It took more than a century for the Chinese to get over the shock. China's imperial system of government, which hadn't changed much in the two thousand years since the Ch'in Empire, collapsed. It wasn't until 1949, when the People's Republic of

China was founded, that the Chinese regained control of their country. They could no longer afford to ignore the rest of the world. The Chinese had to find new answers to the age-old question of what to do about the barbarians.

Today China is a major power. One of every five people on our planet lives in the People's Republic. By the year 2000, the country will have a billion citizens. The population is already very close to the billion mark.

Yet China has the oldest continuing history of any nation on earth. Its past is as long and majestic as the Great Wall, with as many twists and turns.

IN THE BEGINNING

The first real human beings in China lived about 600,000 years ago. Fossils of *Gigantopithecus*, a Latin name for Giant Ape, were dug up at Lan-t'ien in the early 1960s. Though they looked a lot like apes, the Lan-t'ien people were among the first of our species to make tools.

A type of people known as Peking Man lived about a half million years ago. They belonged to what scientists call the Old Stone Age. Remains of forty-five men, women, and children show that Peking Man made rough tools by flaking flints and shaping branches into clubs. These people lived in caves, knew how to use fire, and seem to have had the beginnings of speech. Like *Gigantopithecus*, Peking Man was apelike, with a low forehead, heavy eyebrow ridge, and jutting jaw.

Several types of human beings came and went in the next half million years. Gradually they grew to look less like apes and more like human beings do today. The Upper Cave People, who lived about fifty thousand years ago, marked the first appearance of

Today, one of every five people on our planet lives in China.

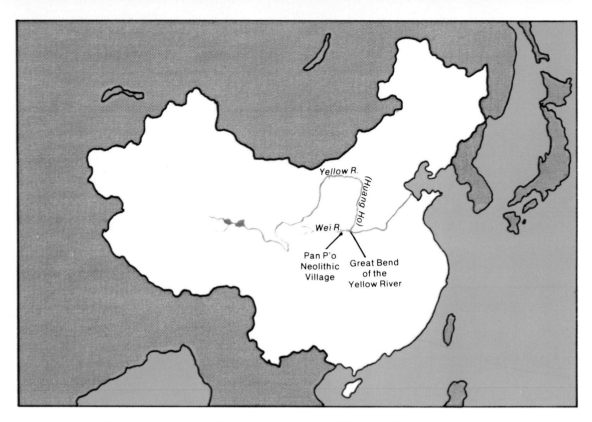

modern human beings—*homo sapiens*—in China. These people fished and hunted, and they gathered roots and fruits to round out their diet.

The Chinese remained hunters and gatherers for the next four hundred centuries or so. Their tools and weapons kept improving. They also developed speech and learned how to make and use fire. Then, about 5000 to 4000 B.C., they discovered how to farm. China moved into a time known as the Neolithic period.

The first farming communities sprang up around the Great Bend of the Yellow River, where the Wei River joins it from the west. Today we call this area the birthplace of Chinese culture. To the north, south, and east, the old hunting and gathering way of life continued for a while. But around the Great Bend, the discovery of farming led to all kinds of advances.

For one thing, people began to live in larger settlements. Villages replaced the scattered caves of earlier times. Whenever a

Above: This painting shows what the Neolithic village of Pan-p'o looked like. Left: The Pan-p'o excavation site.

lot of people live close together, new ideas seem to spring up. Along with the discovery of farming came the invention of pottery and weaving. People started to raise cattle, sheep, horses, pigs, dogs, and chickens.

The most complete remains of a food-producing, Neolithic village can be seen today at Pan-p'o in Shensi Province. This culture, or way of life, lasted from about 4500 to 3000 B.C. The chief crop was a cereal called millet. Enough of it was grown around Pan-p'o to feed at least four hundred people.

It took a high degree of cooperation to grow that much food.

From what we know about the land in those days, the people of Pan-p'o probably had to irrigate their fields. It seems likely that they owned their farms and animals in common and shared the results of their work.

In Neolithic times, people lived in close-knit family groups, or clans. Neighboring clans formed tribes and chose chiefs. Tribes, in turn, joined forces against other tribes.

One such alliance was led by a chief called Huang-ti—the Yellow Emperor. Legends say that he was the founder of Chinese civilization and its first human ruler. Before Huang-ti, so the story goes, the earth was ruled by gods.

Huang-ti was one of the most powerful leaders in the Yellow River area sometime around 2500 B.C. He and the four rulers who came after him presided over China's Golden Age. They set up the ceremonies of government and the sacrifices to be made to the gods, mountains, and streams. They taught the difference between right and wrong and showed the people the correct way to behave.

Legends say that during the reign of the Five Emperors, the government of the world was perfect. The last of the five, Yü, is supposed to have founded the Hsia dynasty sometime around 2000 B.C. A dynasty is a ruling family that stays in power for a fairly long time—usually for several generations. With a couple of exceptions, China was ruled by one dynasty or another for the next four thousand years.

Yü was called the "Great Engineer." He was the first to build large-scale waterworks to control the flooding of the Yellow River. One story says he worked for thirteen years alongside the people, building dams and digging canals, without once going into his house to rest.

The legendary Emperor Yü is said to have been the first to build
large-scale waterworks to control the Yellow River. Over the centuries,
the Chinese have continued to build and maintain levees to keep the
river from flooding the countryside. This is the levee at Cheng-chou.

Since ancient times, in the north of China the right amount of
rain for a good harvest seems to fall only every three or four
years. In between are long dry spells or times of great flooding.
The success or failure of large-scale waterworks has played a big
part in Chinese history since the reign of Yü.

The dynasty that Yü founded lasted about five hundred years.
China was changing from a Neolithic to a Bronze Age culture.
Metal tools replaced stone. Dams, irrigation canals, and other
waterworks led to improvements in farming and stock breeding.
Cities and towns grew up. People started to make carriages and
boats.

In the old days of the village at Pan-p'o, clothes were made of
coarse, loosely woven fabric, and pottery was made by hand. By
the end of the Hsia dynasty, silk culture had been invented, and
weaving had become highly skilled. Fine, smooth pottery was
made on potter's wheels, and bronze vessels began to appear.

THE CHINESE LANGUAGE

The Chinese language is very different from any Western language. It is a *tonal* language. That means that a single Chinese word can be pronounced in several different ways. If the English word "no" were to be pronounced in Mandarin, the national language of China, it could be pronounced in a high, flat, almost sing-song voice; with a rising pronunciation, in much the same way a voice is raised when a question is being asked; with a low, deep voice; or sharply, as if in disapproval.

As you can see, listening to Chinese could be very confusing. Also, there are several different Chinese dialects (regional pronunciations), which makes the language even more confusing. Some dialects have five, six, or even eight tones.

Such big differences might have made it very difficult for people from various regions to understand each other. However, the Chinese language, unlike European languages, was written the same way, and had the same meaning, all over China. Western languages are *phonetic*; that is, the letters used to make up words indicate sound but not meaning. Many Chinese characters, however, are *pictographs*. Anyone who can read Chinese can understand its meaning without knowing how to pronounce it. Therefore, educated people from different parts of China could communicate through writing, if not always through speaking.

The pictographic, or picturelike, origin of Chinese remains clear in some characters that are in use today.

The character for "water" is *shui*. It looks like this:

As you can see, it looks like a picture of several streams running into one river. Thus, the picture represents water.

The character for "big" is *da*. It looks like a stick figure of a big person standing with arms outstretched:

The Chinese also made characters by combining two or more separate characters into one.

The word for "bright" is *ming*:

It is made up of the character for "sun" *(ri)*:

plus the character for "moon" *(yue)*:

Of course, the Chinese language is not limited to simple pictures drawn from observation of the world. The Chinese people, and especially the scholar-officials who governed them for so long, spent thousands of years developing a language that is very descriptive and concrete. In doing so, they have created a body of literature, poetry, philosophy, and history unsurpassed by other cultures.

By Hsia times, Chinese writing had come a long way. As early as 3500 B.C., the Chinese started to make *pictographs*—rough drawings of objects such as the sun, or a house, or a woman. Gradually they combined certain drawings to express ideas. For example, the symbols for "sun" and "moon" written together mean "light" or "bright." These symbols are called *ideographs*. By the end of Hsia times, the written language had several thousand ideographs.

SILK

Chinese legends say that Empress Hsi Ling-shi discovered silk around 2700 B.C. The emperor had ordered her to find out what was wrong with the mulberry trees in his garden. She found them covered with white worms spinning sparkling cocoons. By accident, the empress dropped a cocoon into hot water. A cobweblike mass separated, and the empress discovered it was made from a single, slender thread. Hsi Ling-shi invented the silk reel to spin several fibers into one strong thread. Some say she also invented the first loom for weaving silk fabric.

Whether the legends are true or not, the secret of making silk remained with the Chinese for three thousand years. To discuss silk making with a barbarian was punishable by death. Traders from ancient Persia bought rich silks from Chinese merchants and carried them by caravans across Asia to Damascus for trade to the West. The Romans paid fabulous prices for Chinese silk. Not until A.D. 550, when two monks smuggled silkworm eggs and mulberry seeds out of China, did the secret of silk making reach the West.

SHANG DYNASTY

Sometime in the eighteenth century B.C. the Hsia were defeated by a neighboring tribe called the Shang, who won control over the middle and lower territories of the Yellow River.

The Shang dynasty marks the beginning of documented Chinese history. Unlike the Hsia dynasty before it, the Shang dynasty left some written records as evidence of what the society and culture were like. Also, the tombs and other remains found in Anyang County, once the Shang capital, tell us a lot about life in those days.

The simple people—that is, most Chinese—lived in pit dwellings that hadn't changed much from the Neolithic houses at Pan-p'o. Their floors were sunk a few feet (about one meter) below ground level, and they were topped with beehive-shaped roofs. Most people, as in Neolithic times, farmed the land. The growing use of bronze made better weapons and tools possible. Wheeled carts and chariots became common in Shang times. These developments led to increased wealth and the growth of trade. Under the Shang, people started to use cowrie shells as money.

Farming improved, and workers became highly skilled in pottery, weaving, toolmaking, and other crafts and trades. The Shang dynasty is famous for the fabulous bronzes its workers produced. Huge, decorated vessels were used for religious ceremonies. Bronze wine cups, weapons, ornaments, and plates also have been found. To this day, no one has bettered the high standard of skill and beauty practiced by Shang bronze workers.

The workers did not benefit much from their own labor, however. Instead, all surplus, or leftover, wealth belonged to the kings, warriors, and priests who formed the ruling class.

The fabulous bronzes produced by Shang dynasty workers include this elaborate ritual wine pitcher (above) and a huge ritual vessel decorated with a human face.

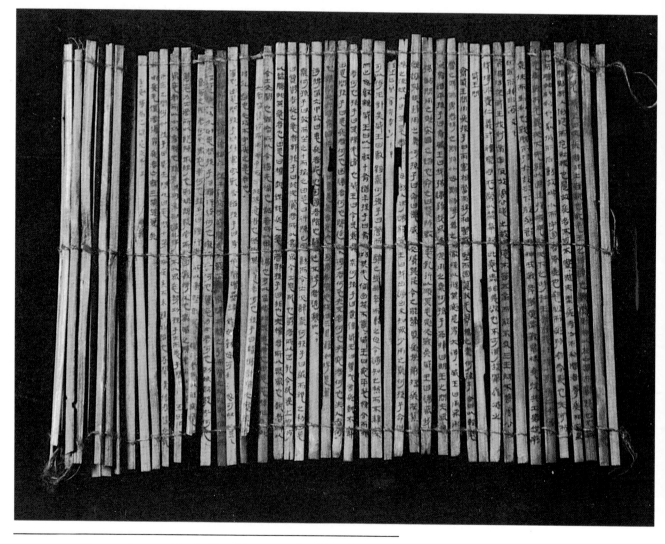

Shang rulers read books like this one, made of bamboo strips.

These people lived in cities surrounded by walls as thick as fifty-five feet (seventeen meters) at the base. Their beautiful houses and palaces were built by workers and slaves. The rulers wore fine cloth woven from silk and flax and read books made of bamboo strips and wooden tablets.

Shang rulers worshiped their ancestors and other spirits. When they wanted to know whether rain would fall or war would come, they wrote their questions to the gods on tortoise shells or the shoulder bones of animals. The bones were then heated. Priests studied the pattern of the heat cracks to find the spirits' answers. In one pit at Anyang, some eighteen thousand of these "dragon bones" were found.

When Shang rulers died, they were buried with the things they would need in the next world, from chariots, gold, and jade to slaves. In one tomb at Anyang, scientists discovered the remains of seventy slaves who were buried alive when their owner died.

The Shang dynasty lasted about five hundred years. During this time, the Shang developed many of the patterns that would influence Chinese culture and society for several thousand years to come. They developed a ruling aristocracy based on military power and education; a secretarial class of men whose duty was to keep and interpret written records; and the ability to control and move large numbers of people for state projects. They also developed the idea of Chinese culture as the center of the world, an idea that would stay with the Chinese throughout the rest of their long history.

Throughout their reign, Shang rulers fought many wars with neighboring tribes. For centuries, Shang chariots and bronze weapons were used to beat back the invaders. But all those wars drained the country and put heavy burdens on the common people. Finally, late in the twelfth century B.C., the slaves of the Shang revolted. At just the same time, the tribe of Chou attacked the Shang from west of the Great Bend. Many Shang slaves crossed over to the Chou, and the Shang dynasty collapsed. In 1122 B.C., the Chou king burned the royal palace and started his own dynasty.

Chou dynasty workers continued the Shang tradition of bronze making. This set of sacrificial vessels is said to have come from a tomb at Feng-Hsiang in Shensi Province.

Chapter 2

THE CHOU DYNASTY

WESTERN CHOU

The Chou family ruled China for the next nine centuries (1122-221 B.C.) — longer than any other dynasty in Chinese history. These barbarians from the west were indeed less civilized at first than the Shang. But they took over many features of the Shang way of life, such as farming, writing, and bronze making. Gradually the Chou barbarians were absorbed into Chinese culture.

The king of the Chou passed out lands as *fiefs*, or private estates, to the royal princes. The princes became *vassals* of the king. They had to promise to send troops to the king's army and to protect the court. The vassals sent regular tributes—gifts of gold, grain, and other valuables—to the king of Chou. Every so often, the royal princes had to go to the capital and take part in ceremonies that showed how great the king was and how lowly they were compared to him. In return for all this, the king did not meddle in the princes' kingdoms. Within their own states, the vassals could pretty much rule as they pleased.

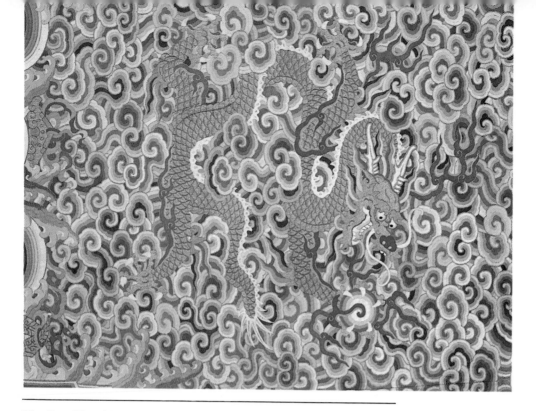

The first Chou king's dragon symbol was used by emperors throughout the centuries to denote power, knowledge, fertility, and well-being. The dragon shown here is one of twelve that decorate a Ch'ing emperor's robe.

The first Chou king called himself the Son of Heaven. His symbol was the dragon, and no one else was permitted to use it. He alone could give or take away fiefs. He also had special duties to the gods. The Son of Heaven was the only person in China who could perform the ceremonies and sacrifices the Chinese thought were needed for good weather and rich harvests.

The Son of Heaven was supposed to set an example for his subjects. If he behaved well and lived a good life, it was said, his subjects would obey him and do the same, and the country would prosper. But if trouble struck the Central Kingdom—whether drought, flood, or a slave revolt—it was the king's fault. Disasters were taken as a sign that he had done something bad, or had fallen from grace. Heaven would then take back its support, or *mandate*, from the fallen king and give it to a more deserving person.

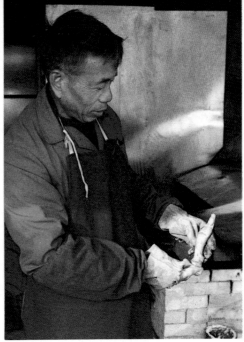

*Far left:
A Chou dynasty
bronze food vessel
Left: An artisan
of today
demonstrates the
traditional
lost-wax-process
technique of
bronze casting
developed during
the Chou dynasty.*

Early Chinese historians used this *mandate of heaven* idea to explain why it was right for the Chou to overthrow the Shang dynasty. Shang rulers behaved so badly, they wrote, that heaven withdrew its mandate and gave it to the more worthy Chou. An ancient Chinese proverb says: "He who succeeds becomes emperor. He who fails is a bandit."

In the early days of the Chou, the royal princes and the ruling class were the only people who were educated. They spent a lot of time learning the rules and ceremonies that were proper to their rank. They also studied arithmetic, poetry, and music. From the ruling class came ministers and counselors in times of peace and generals in times of war.

Some Chinese rulers owned thousands of slaves. Human life was cheap in those days. Five slaves were worth one horse and one hank (coiled length) of silk. Slave labor built the palaces, cities, towns, and waterworks of the Chou dynasty. Chou towns were full of slaves who were craft workers. They wove silk of the finest quality and made bronzes equal to those of the Shang dynasty.

But as in earlier times, most people in China tilled the soil. The growth in farming led to a huge rise in population. This meant there were more workers to clear more land and build the canals and ditches to irrigate it. The range of crops included wheat, maize, rice, beans, fruits, and many other foods.

In the north and west, the growth of stock breeding gave rise to wandering tribes of mountain herders. These hardy, independent people were not so easily ruled as the farmers in the Great Bend area. Gradually they grew strong enough to start making raids on the more settled communities to the east.

EASTERN CHOU

In 770 B.C., western barbarians overran the Chou capital at Hao. The king and his court moved east to Loyang. The Eastern Chou dynasty lasted another five hundred years or so. But for much of that time, the Chou were in power in name only.

During the Eastern Chou period, iron replaced bronze in China. Iron was easier to work with, there was more of it, and it made better tools. More land was cleared and farmed, and the vassal states grew richer and stronger. Dozens of them declared their independence from the king of Chou and started fighting among themselves.

With the rise of these local princes, a new class of people appeared in China. The *scholars*, like the nobles and priests, could read and write. They wandered from state to state offering their services. Scholars advised local princes on affairs of state and helped to run the government. They also taught the princes how to perform the all-important ceremonies.

Some scholars even started to teach students from among the

This jade ornament with a griffin in the center was made during the Eastern Chou dynasty.

common people. For the first time in Chinese history, education spread beyond the ranks of the wealthy ruling classes. But educated Chinese were still vastly outnumbered by the peasants.

WARRING STATES

During the Warring States period (481-221 B.C.), farming and water control improved. More grain led to increased trade and the growth of cities packed with merchants and craft workers. Late in the period, the Chinese started to use bronze coins with holes in the middle. They also began to eat with chopsticks.

The Chinese culture—its written and spoken language, farming methods, and other ways of life—spread south to the Yangtze River. Seven kingdoms emerged from the struggles among the warring princes. Each kingdom raised large troops of foot soldiers, drawn from the rising number of peasants. The northern states, taking a hint from their barbarian neighbors, added horse soldiers, or cavalry, to their ranks.

A Confucian temple

Chapter 3

THE HUNDRED SCHOOLS OF THOUGHT

Centuries of war and unrest were very hard on the Chinese people. Many teachers and philosophers asked questions and sought answers in those troubled times. There were so many wandering scholars that historians have called this period the time of the Hundred Schools of Thought.

CONFUCIANISM

Confucius (551-479 B.C.) was a wandering scholar from the state of Lu. He worried about China's troubles. All those warring kingdoms wouldn't even recognize the Son of Heaven as their rightful ruler. Confucius thought this state of things spelled disaster. He puzzled over what had gone wrong and how China could get back on the right path. In doing so, he founded a tradition that would have enormous influence over how subsequent rulers and officials would organize and govern China. The Confucian tradition, despite many different interpretations and schools of thought, would dominate Chinese society for more than twenty-four hundred years.

Confucius taught a code of behavior rather than a religion. It was a practical code, one that could be applied to everyday life at all levels of Chinese government and society. Confucius thought that if everyone understood his or her place in the world, and what was expected by others, then peace and harmony would rule. He singled out five relationships for people to understand: between husband and wife, father and son, older and younger brother, friend and friend, and ruler and ruled.

Confucius taught that people should behave honorably toward family members and others in the community. Loyalty, respect, sincerity, and courtesy were highly valued. "Do not do to others," he wrote, "what you would not want them to do to you."

The ruler, as the father of his people and the highest authority in the land, was supposed to set an outstanding example. If he were good, wise, dignified, and performed the proper ceremonies, his people would behave likewise. But a dishonest, harsh, or wicked ruler could not expect loyalty from his ministers or his people.

The ruler was the Son of Heaven as well as the father of the kingdom. His duty as a good son was to make offerings and sacrifices to heaven for the well-being of his people.

Confucius thought that government positions should be earned by education and talent, not by birth. The ruler, he said, should set up schools for the nobles to teach brotherly love, respect, and humility.

Confucius went from court to court, trying to spread his ideas among the upper classes. But he couldn't find a prince who would put his teachings into practice. Finally he gave up talking to princes and spent the last years of his life teaching a small group of followers.

Confucius's teachings were collected in a group of books called the *Confucian Classics*. They didn't catch on right away. As you will see, Confucius had a lot of competition. But within a few hundred years, the *Confucian Classics* became the official teaching of the state, and the basis of the Chinese social system.

Mencius was yet another teacher in those days. A follower of Confucius, he lived about a hundred years after the master. Like Confucius, Mencius served in a government post. Mencius taught that there were two kinds of people. *Superior* people worked with their heads and were meant to rule. *Inferior* people worked with their hands and were meant to be ruled. The Confucian scholars ranked the common people of China according to their value in society. Farmers were at the top of the heap, because their work was the backbone of the state. Artisans, or craft workers, came next. Merchants were low on the totem pole. They didn't produce anything with their labor, and were thought of as parasites. Soldiers were the only group rated lower and the Confucians thought so little of them that they placed them outside and below normal society.

Both Confucius and Mencius were teachers. Each spent his life pursuing some kind of government post from which he could put his teachings into practice. There was a third man in the Confucian tradition, however, who was very much involved in government. His ideas became very influential for that reason. His name was Hsun-tzu, and he was the first of China's "scholar-officials." These men combined a high standard of education with government service, and their ideas formed the basis of Chinese government for the next two thousand years.

Hsun-tzu (298-238 B.C.) was considered the most educated man of his time, as were Confucius and Mencius before him. He also spent much of his life in the service of his state. He taught that governments had to be strong because people were basically bad. The power of the state was needed to control them in order to make them good. Hsun-tzu's opinion was very different from that of Mencius, who believed that people were basically good and did not need to be oppressed and controlled by a strong government.

Hsun-tzu also taught that culture, by which he meant the observance of ceremonies and rituals guiding people's behavior, was mankind's highest achievement. But culture was always threatened by people's evil nature. Thus, strong government was necessary in order to make sure that ceremonies and rituals were maintained.

Hsun-tzu's ideas enjoyed more immediate influence than did the ideas of Confucius and Mencius. Some of his students used his ideas to bring about the first Chinese empire, the Ch'in.

TAOISM

In contrast to the schools of practical political and social philosophy established by Confucius and his followers, there existed a religion based on the *Tao*, or natural way to truth. Legends say that Lao-tzu (575-485? B.C.) was the first great teacher of Taoism, although no one has ever proved that he actually lived. But the ideas collected in the *Tao Te Ching*, or the *Classic of the Way and Virtue*, won a lot of followers in the last years of the Chou dynasty.

Taoists didn't care much for the fancy ceremonies or ideas of government put forward by Confucius, Mencius, or Hsun-tzu. They thought that living simply, in harmony with nature, was the

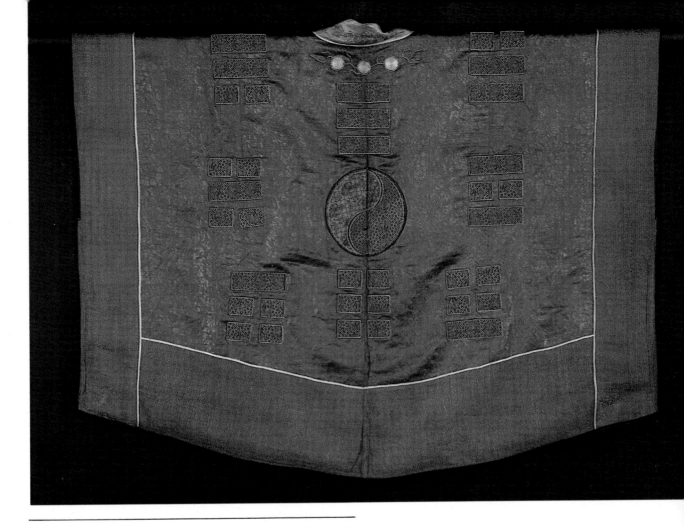

A Taoist priest's robe of blue and red brocade

way people could find peace. For Taoists, happiness was to be achieved through nature, while for Confucians, happiness was achieved by concentrating on and ordering society. Taoists believed that truth had to be felt rather than taught. No amount of learning could help a person find peace. Followers of this mystical religion tended to withdraw from public life because they saw no purpose in being involved with governments, or even with other people. "Those who strive for nothing cannot be disappointed" was one favorite Taoist saying.

MOHISM

The *Mohists,* followers of Mo-tzu (479-438 B.C.), looked at things differently. While Confucius emphasized duty to one's family, Mohists believed in universal love. While Taoists ignored the sad state of China's peasants, Mohists taught that it was criminal for some people to live in luxury as long as there was not enough food and clothing for all.

YIN AND YANG

The cycle of floods and droughts in China had a lot to do with how the ancient Chinese viewed the world. The earliest religions were concerned with maintaining a balance between the two great forces of nature, called yin and yang. Yin was dark and female; yang was light and male. Yin stood for the earth; yang, for the sky. One followed the other, like night and day. Harmony between yin and yang was thought necessary for people's well-being.

LEGALISM

Of all the schools of thought that sprouted around the fifth and fourth centuries B.C., the *Legalists* won the most immediate success. Legalists said that human nature was basically bad, and that strong laws and armies were necessary to keep people in line. They believed that everyone should do productive work. Merchants and scholars were useless, said the Legalists, because they didn't produce anything. Music, poetry, philosophy, and history were worthless. Farming and soldiering were what counted in a prosperous kingdom.

Chapter 4

THE CH'IN DYNASTY

Shang Yang (400-338 B.C.) was an important Legalist. In 361 B.C. he became the chief minister to the king of Ch'in, a country in the Wei River valley in northwest China.

The Legalists of Ch'in built a strong state and a mighty army. They stripped power from the old noble families and gave it to generals who proved their worth in battle. New lands captured in war were governed by the state, not by royal princes.

One by one, the Ch'in conquered the other six Chinese kingdoms, which had been too busy fighting among themselves to join forces against their common enemy. After two hundred years of war, China for the first time became united under a central government. Emperor Shih Huang-ti—the man who built the Great Wall—ruled a state that stretched from the Mongolian Plateau to the Yangtze River basin. From there his armies pushed south to Vietnam and the coast near Canton.

Though the Ch'in dynasty lasted only fifteen years, the imperial system of government developed by the Ch'in persisted for two thousand years.

The Ch'in got rid of the vassal states and divided China into provinces and counties. These were ruled by officials from the central government. They had to earn their titles and could not pass them on to their offspring.

Governors collected taxes in their provinces and enforced the law. They also drafted peasants for the army and for public works, such as building the Great Wall. Local army commanders made sure the governors did their jobs.

The Ch'in set up one system of weights, measures, and coins for the entire empire. They also built a vast network of roads and simplified the written language.

Farmers were given more rights to their land than ever before, but they were also heavily taxed. Scholars suffered greatly under the Ch'in. After one trial, 460 scholars were buried alive. Throughout China, soldiers tore down libraries and made huge bonfires of books.

Ch'in armies, made up of hundreds of thousands of peasants, were on the march day and night. Still more peasants were drafted to dig irrigation canals and build the Great Wall. The farmers were heavily taxed to pay for all the wars and public works. Some sold themselves and their children into slavery. In addition, Ch'in laws were very strict, with harsh penalties for even the smallest crimes.

The success of the Ch'in empire depended on the efforts of the first emperor of China, Shih Huang-ti, and the Legalist advisers who had helped him to achieve power. With his death in 209 B.C., the Ch'in state fell into civil war. After a short but terrible period of warfare, the peasant revolt of 206 B.C. brought down the Ch'in dynasty. China endured a further period of great disorder until 202 B.C., when the Han dynasty was established.

The excavated terra-cotta army shown above was buried in the tomb of Ch'in emperor
Shih Huang-ti in 209 B.C. to accompany and protect his spirit into the next world.
The painting below, a depiction of the peasant revolt of 206 B.C. that brought
down the Ch'in dynasty, is exhibited in the Peking Museum of Natural History.

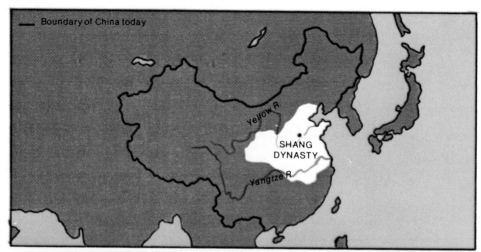

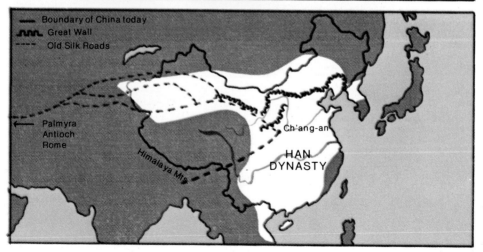

Chapter 5

THE HAN DYNASTY

Under Han rulers (202 B.C.-A.D. 221), China more than doubled in size. At its peak, the Han dynasty equaled the Roman Empire in brilliance and military power. To this day, native Chinese call themselves "Han people" to distinguish themselves from minority groups of "barbarian" descent.

Han emperors opened a trade route to the West. Caravans followed the Old Silk Roads from northwest China to India, Persia, and the Mediterranean countries. Chinese silk was highly prized throughout the world. The barbarian demand for silk was much greater than China's interest in the ivory, perfume, and jewels the West had to offer. But Western horses were greatly valued in China.

The Han dynasty came to power on a wave of peasant revolt. The first emperors took steps to improve life for the common people. Taxes were cut, and the harsh laws of the Ch'in taken off the books. People who had sold themselves as slaves were freed, and Ch'in soldiers were told to go back to their farms.

The Han built more waterworks and cleared more land for farming. The supply of grain and silk increased. So did the population.

With the ban on books lifted, scholars began to restore the *Confucian Classics.* In the first century of Han rule, the teachings of Confucius and his followers became the official word of the state. The Han started the system in which anyone who wanted to be in the government had to pass a series of tests on the *Confucian Classics.* From Han times until the twentieth century, the most important way to get ahead in China was to do well on these civil service tests.

Only the sons of wealthy and noble families were allowed to take the exams in Han times. It wasn't until two dynasties later — nearly nine hundred years — that the civil service system was opened to young men from all classes. But whatever class they came from, the government officials who emerged from the civil service tests became the new ruling group in China — the *mandarins.* The teachings of Confucius and his followers became the basis of the Chinese system of government and education for the next two thousand years.

The Chinese made many advances during the Han dynasty. Papermaking spread from China to Japan, Korea, India, and Arabia — a thousand years before it was introduced in Europe. The first dictionaries and a general history of China were written under the Han, as well as many books on medicine and mathematics. Chang Heng, an astronomer, mathematician, and poet, invented a seismograph. It showed whenever a region in China was rocked by an earthquake.

The fierce attacks of the barbarian Huns did not stop when the Han took over. The emperors tried to handle the problem in several different ways. At first, they tried to win over the Huns by offering to let their leaders marry Chinese princesses. At other times, the Chinese waged war on the Huns. The Han dynasty

Among the many Chinese inventions of the Han dynasty was the seismograph (above), invented by Chang Heng sixteen hundred years before the Western world produced its first seismograph. When slightly shaken by an earth tremor, the rod inside the seismograph caused one of the dragons to open its mouth and drop a bronze ball into the mouth of one of the toads squatting below.

Also during the Han dynasty, the Chinese invented papermaking. The twentieth-century artisan shown below is carrying on the ancient tradition.

ACUPUNCTURE

Acupuncture—a method of relieving pain and treating illness—was perfected during Han times. Needles inserted at certain points on the body are thought to cure all sorts of illnesses, from asthma to ulcers, from arthritis to poor eyesight. The Chinese believe that a life-force flows through the body along definite paths. When the flow is blocked, or when the forces of yin and yang are out of balance in the body, the needles are used to restore good health. Chinese doctors today can perform major surgery with no anesthetic but acupuncture. The patient remains conscious but feels little or no pain.

Medical students in ancient China tested their acupuncture skills on bronze models such as this one.

invited neighboring barbarian tribes to join with them in attacking their common enemy.

Embassies from these allied tribes went to the Han capital bearing horses, gold, and other valuables, which the Chinese called "tribute." The barbarians returned home with bolts of silk and other Chinese goods. In time, the Chinese took this tribute system as a sign that the barbarian allies recognized the Son of Heaven as their superior and lord—even when this wasn't the case. To the barbarians, the exchange of gifts was a ceremony that sealed an alliance between equals.

The long and costly wars against the Huns took their toll on the Chinese common people, as usual. Because large numbers of peasants were drafted into the army, farmland was not cared for. People starved in times of flood and drought. Taxes were raised to pay for the wars. Peasants who couldn't pay lost their land to government officials, who didn't have to pay taxes.

As the landlords grew in power and wealth, they started to fight each other. Sometimes they even plotted against the emperor. The peasants formed secret societies to plot against the landlords. The emperor sent armies to put down peasant rebellions. But the army generals began to get their own ideas about seizing power.

These problems at home, plus continued attacks by the Huns, enabled one of the Han officials, Wang Mang, to seize power and temporarily end Han rule at the end of the first century B.C. But the Han regained power in A.D. 25 and kept it until 221. At first they took measures to improve things for the peasants. But as time went on, the same old pattern repeated itself. The landlords grew richer and the peasants got poorer. The generals sent to put down peasant revolts seized power for themselves. Different groups at court plotted against each other while the barbarians kept up their attacks.

Doors leading to the Han tombs (left) and this Han tomb stone carving (below) can be seen today at Cheng-chou.

AGE OF DISUNITY

Widespread revolt brought down the Han in A.D. 221. China broke up into smaller kingdoms, each ruled by a warlord. For almost four centuries, war and natural disasters reigned in China. Historians call this period the Age of Disunity.

As in the Warring States period, the Chinese people sought relief from their suffering in a new set of beliefs. A religion called Buddhism spread from India to the Central Kingdom in the third century A.D. and attracted many followers during the next few centuries.

CHANG CH'IEN—THE MAN WHO DISCOVERED EUROPE

In 138 B.C. Wu Ti, the greatest of the Han emperors, heard of a tribe to the west that had been defeated by the Hun barbarians. The emperor decided to seek out this tribe and propose an alliance against the Huns. He ordered General Chang Ch'ien and a hundred followers to find the land of the Ta Yueh Chi.

Almost at once, Chang Ch'ien was captured. The Huns kept him prisoner for ten years. When Chang Ch'ien finally escaped, he fled westward, not east toward China.

Chang Ch'ien caught up with the Ta Yueh Chi in what is now Afghanistan. Though he stayed with them a year, he failed to persuade them to join in the war against the Huns. Chang Ch'ien was recaptured by the Huns on his way back to China and spent yet another year in captivity. He finally returned to the emperor twelve years after he had set out. With him were a barbarian wife and only one of his original hundred followers.

Though Chang Ch'ien failed to perform his mission, he had reached the outer fringes of the Western world. He discovered the West for China a thousand years before the West discovered the Central Kingdom.

This master craftsman is demonstrating the ancient Chinese art of carving porcelain. Though fine porcelain wasn't perfected until about A.D. 700, skilled Chinese artisans have been making pottery since prehistoric times.

A Buddhist temple in a lovely hillside setting

A detail from a Buddhist priest's robe made of silk, metal thread, and peacock feathers

BUDDHISM

Buddhism teaches that life is suffering. It also preaches reincarnation—that is, when a person dies, the soul is reborn in a new body. A person's misery will be endless, say the Buddhists, until he learns to rid himself of all earthly desires and attachments. This could take many lifetimes. But the Buddhists offer hope that the soul can finally learn its lesson and free itself from the cycle of rebirth. The Buddhists' goal is to reach *nirvana*—a state of heavenly peace in which the soul is released from the pain and suffering of earthly life and becomes one with the universe.

By the sixth century A.D. Buddhism was widely accepted in China. The new religion existed side by side with Confucianism and Taoism. Many Chinese considered these different schools of thought as "three ways to one goal."

47

A statue of Buddha in the White Horse Monastery at Sian

BUDDHA

Gautama Buddha, the founder of the religion of Buddhism, was a prince of northern India. He was born about 563 B.C. Legends say that he lived a sheltered life when he was growing up. The first time he saw poverty, sickness, and death, Gautama began to question the purpose of being alive. He left his home and family to search for truth. After wandering for many years, he found the answers he sought. Gautama became the Buddha, or "Enlightened One," and his soul was finally at peace.

Buddha had many followers, and his teachings spread throughout India and central Asia. Traders and missionaries carried Buddhism with them over caravan routes to China toward the end of the third century A.D.

The Lungmen Caves near Loyang, begun in A.D. 495, have more than
a hundred thousand statues of all sizes. In one hall alone, there are ten thousand
statues of Buddha. Shown here are some of the "guardians" of the caves.

To show their scorn for working with their hands, the mandarins let their fingernails grow several inches long. Many of them wore nail guards to prevent accidental breakage of the long nails. Servants followed the mandarins around with hand pillows on which the mandarins could rest their nails. Even into the twentieth century, learned men, or those with high government positions, did not work with their hands. This picture, taken in 1914, shows a man with nails twenty-six inches long. To protect them at night, he slipped them into the bamboo casings.

THE MANDARINS

Chinese culture held together in the Age of Disunity, despite famine, wars, and widespread suffering. A barbarian tribe called the Topa overran the north. But they were quickly absorbed by their civilized conquests. The Topa rulers depended on the Chinese mandarins, or scholar-officials, to run things for them. The barbarians soon began using the Chinese language, imitating Chinese clothing styles, and following other Chinese customs.

Some mandarins grew lazy and corrupt. They promoted Mencius's idea that people who worked with their heads were superior to those who worked with their hands.

Pressure from the barbarians to the north sent many Chinese streaming south across the Yangtze River; thus Chinese culture continued to spread. Better farming conditions in the south led to the rise of the Sui Kingdom, which finally reunited China in A.D. 589 and ushered in the Second Empire.

Chapter 6

THE SECOND EMPIRE

SUI DYNASTY

The new Son of Heaven cut taxes, gave public lands to the peasants, rewrote laws, and made other reforms. But the Sui dynasty (589-618) followed the classic pattern of the rise and fall of Chinese ruling families. The reforms of the early days were undone by corruption and peasant abuse, and the dynasty lost the "mandate of heaven."

The second Sui emperor, Yang Ti, had grand plans for China. But he destroyed almost half the labor force trying to accomplish them. Yang Ti built the Grand Canal to link the Yellow, Huai, and Yangtze rivers. The canal joined the rich rice lands of the Yangtze Valley in the south with the northern regions. It was of great benefit in unifying China. But other of Yang Ti's projects were disastrous. He waged and lost a war in Korea that put almost a million Chinese peasants to flight. Finally he was killed by army officers. In 618, a peasant rebel put his father on the dragon throne and founded the T'ang dynasty.

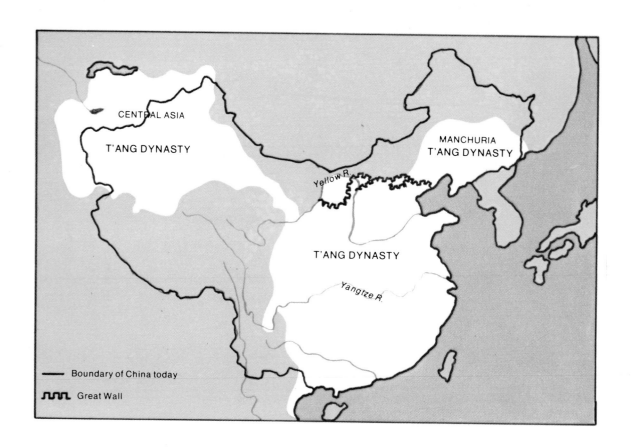

- — Boundary of China today
- ♒ Great Wall

T'ANG DYNASTY

At the height of T'ang power, in the decades before 750, China was the largest country in the world. It stretched west through central Asia as far as the Pamir Mountains, and included Mongolia and Manchuria in the north. Tibet and Korea were vassal states. Chinese influence spread throughout Asia and was especially strong in Japan. Trade and art flourished, and Buddhism in China reached its peak.

The first T'ang emperor, Li Shih-min, was a skilled general, governor, and scholar. He learned enough from studying other dynasties not to burden the farmers with heavy taxes and forced labor. He felt it was best for China if the peasants were as well off as possible. A system was devised in which land taken by the government from large landowners was rented to peasants. This so-called equal field system resulted in greater food production and thus greater wealth for the T'ang empire. The equal field system, together with the building of irrigation works, effective government administration, and the reopening of trade with the outside world, made the T'ang empire the richest that China had yet known.

Exams for government positions were opened to all ranks except merchants and outcast groups. Almost anyone who could afford an education could take the tests. This reform sounds better than it actually worked out. Most peasants could not pay for schooling. Still, thousands of students gathered in the provinces to take the civil service tests. Those who passed went on to the capital for another round of tests.

The T'ang enlarged the imperial college and built schools in the provinces. The colleges taught the Confucian ideas of loyalty to authority, respect for family and tradition, and honorable behavior. They turned out administrators trained in Confucian thought to rule the huge empire.

The emperor and his council still headed the government. They organized China into provinces and districts. Local officials collected taxes, promoted farming and public works, and saw to it that laws were obeyed.

The mandarins themselves did not have to pay taxes, join the army, or donate labor to the state. They were above the law. Power and wealth stayed in the same educated hands as the years went by.

China's system of government was not perfect. The outlook of those who moved up in the ranks of the Confucian civil service was narrow-minded and ill suited to cope with change or suggest

Among the beautiful works produced by T'ang artisans are this glazed earthenware tomb figure of a Heavenly Guardian (left) and a gilt bronze lotus flower (right).

new ways of doing things. Still, the civil service system helped to unify and build the Chinese empire in T'ang times. And it formed the basis of Chinese life until the twentieth century.

The first hundred years of T'ang rule were peaceful. China carried on brisk trade with other nations. Though there was still a big gap between rich and poor, the peasants were better off than they had been for some time. Cities flourished, too. T'ang artisans produced gorgeous pottery, silk, and other handicrafts that are still admired today.

*A wall painting
in the tomb of
the Empress Wu,
China's only female
Son of Heaven*

The T'ang dynasty boasts China's only female Son of Heaven,
the Empress Wu. She was married to Emperor Kao-tsung, who
was a weak and lazy ruler. Wu governed for the emperor and
their son for forty years before she took the imperial title herself
in 690. She sought peace with her neighbors and disbanded
hundreds of thousands of troops. Wu encouraged farming and silk
production and took steps to help the peasants.

The empress was a devout Buddhist. Under her, the religion
reached its peak. Buddhist images—in beautiful sculptures and
paintings—spread all over China. Other religions came to China
at this time. Christians, Moslems, and Jews all practiced their
faiths in the Central Kingdom. But Buddhism had by far the
strongest hold on Chinese souls.

This pavilion in Szechwan Province commemorates the T'ang dynasty poet Tu Fu.

Empress Wu's grandson, Hsuan-tsung (more commonly known to the Chinese as Ming Huang, or "Brilliant Emperor") presided over the climax and decline of the T'ang empire. A lover of poetry, he gradually ignored his obligation to rule the country in favor of spending his time as a patron of the arts. Among those poets who enjoyed his favor were Li Po (701-762) and Tu Fu (712-770). Li Po wrote about nature, friendship, and immortality. He was a man greatly influenced by the Taoist religion. Tu Fu, on the other hand, wrote about the darker side of Chinese life—corrupt officials, warfare, and the suffering of the poor. Tu Fu is considered by many to be the greatest poet in Chinese history, and the T'ang period stands out as the high point of Chinese poetry.

Although Hsuan-tsung's reign (712-756) marked the height of T'ang culture, it also marked the beginning of the decline in T'ang power and influence. The emperor's lack of interest in official business, corruption, increasing pressures from barbarians, and the growing independence of T'ang military officers all added up to trouble for the empire.

In 755 a barbarian general in the service of the T'ang, An Lu-shan, led an uprising that caused Emperor Hsuan-tsung to flee the capital. An Lu-shan declared himself emperor, but his reign was to be short-lived. By 757 he was dead and the rebellion was over. But the T'ang dynasty had been permanently damaged. Although it would not officially end for another 150 years, it was crippled and no measures could help it to regain its former glory.

Some of the steps taken to try to restore the T'ang were desperate indeed. The most notable was the attempted destruction of the Buddhist religion.

By the early 800s, the T'ang decided that Buddhism in China was becoming a threat. Monasteries were taking too many workers away from farms. Monks and nuns did not marry, and so the labor force was not growing as fast as the T'ang would have liked. The monasteries, which also served as inns, hospitals, and even public baths, did not have to pay taxes. Over the years, they amassed a great deal of wealth and land.

In the 840s, a Taoist emperor broke the back of Buddhism in China. Buddhism wasn't outlawed. But more than four thousand monasteries and forty thousand shrines were destroyed. A quarter of a million monks, nuns, and their servants were sent back to the farms—and the tax rolls.

After almost a century of peasant revolts and fights among the generals, the T'ang fell in 907.

THE FIVE DYNASTIES

In the Five Dynasties period (907-960), warlords took over once again. South China split into ten states, and a series of barbarian families ruled in the north.

Finally an army general, Chao K'uang-yin, seized power in the south and set up a stable government. Within twenty years, north and south China were reunited under the Sung dynasty.

The thirteen-story Pagoda of Six Harmonies in Hangchou was built in 970, during the Sung dynasty.

Chapter 7

THE SUNG DYNASTY

The Sung (960-1280) reduced the power of the viceroys and built a strong central government that relied on the civil service exam system for its officials. In general, the Sung tried compromising with the northern barbarians instead of fighting them. Most people in China were thoroughly sick of war.

More land was cleared in the Sung period. Water control projects and improvements in farming increased the food supply. In turn, the population doubled to 100 million by the end of the dynasty.

Though farming improved, peasant life was still miserable. Like rulers before them, the Sung passed new laws to help the common people. But soon they were repealed, and the familiar pattern repeated itself.

Barbarian Kin armies captured Kaifeng, the Sung capital, in 1126. The emperor's son fled south to Hangchou, and finally made peace with the Kin.

Once again, China was divided into north and south. The Kin ruled from the Huai River northward. The Sung held on to the Yangtze Valley and the southern regions.

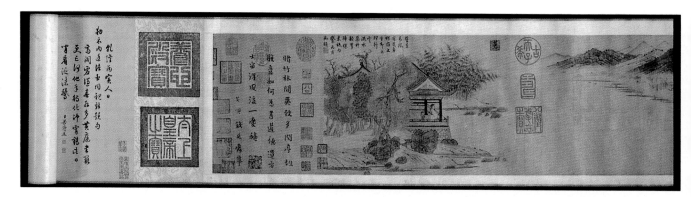

The left and right halves of this handscroll titled Wang Hsi-chih Watching Geese *show the high artistic level reached by Southern Sung dynasty painters.*

EXAM SYSTEM UNDER THE SUNG

Before the Sung dynasty, civil service exams were not given on a regular basis. Under the Sung, the exams were held every three years. Attempts were made to prevent bribery and playing favorites—in general, to keep the system fair. The students came from a broader range of social classes than ever before. Still, about half of the applicants were from mandarin families.

Thousands competed for what amounted to only two hundred government appointments a year. The tests were very difficult. Applicants had to spend seven days and nights in one small room. Some went crazy or died of exhaustion. Those who succeeded sometimes waited years more for a government job. Once a scholar became a district official, however, usually he also became very rich.

Imperial astronomer Su Sung designed this "False Sky Observatory" during the Sung dynasty. Astronomy students sat in the chair suspended in this spherical tent and learned about the movements of the heavens. The bamboo frame was turned from the outside, and light shone in through pinholes that represented the positions of stars.

Though most authorities agree that the Chinese invented the compass in the early 1100s, this magnetic spoon developed in the Han dynasty may have been the world's first compass. The spoon is carved from lodestone, a magnetic iron ore. When spun on the bronze board, the spoon always points south.

TRADE

The Southern Sung dynasty (1127-1200), turned China into a seagoing nation. Instead of the outposts along the Old Silk Roads, the coastal ports of east China became the main points of contact between the Central Kingdom and the outside world. Improvements in navigation fostered the growth of Chinese sea trade. The Chinese first used the compass in the early 1100s, decades before it appeared in Europe. Chinese merchant ships sailed to Southeast Asia, India, the East Indies, and later as far as Africa.

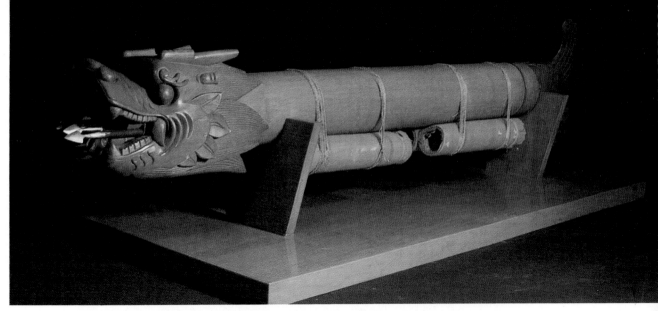

The Chinese discovered gunpowder by accident during the T'ang period. Inventors trying to find a long-life potion for the emperor combined a series of minerals, only to have the mixture explode in their faces (below). At first the Chinese used gunpowder only for fireworks. But during the Sung period, the first military rockets were developed. By the eleventh century, the Chinese had invented a kind of hand grenade and a number of missiles. The two-stage rocket shown above, invented in the thirteenth century, was used in naval warfare.

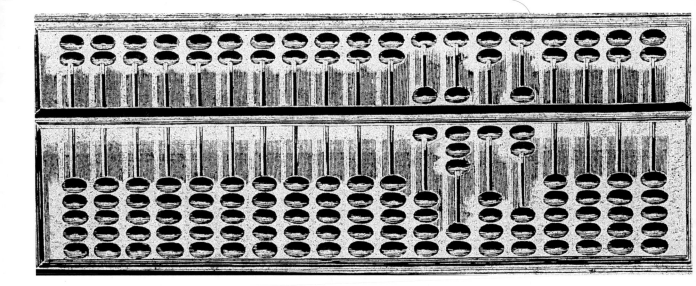

The abacus, invented by the Southern Sung, can be used to add, subtract, multiply, divide, and solve other mathematics problems. It consists of several columns of beads, separated by a crossbar. From right to left, the columns stand for the ones place, the tens place, the hundreds place, and so on. The beads above the crossbar each represent five and those below the bar, one. Math problems are worked by moving beads toward and away from the crossbar.

Other developments fueled the explosion of trade. The Yangtze Valley and southern China generally have better farmlands and more rainfall than northern China. The central and southern provinces were the best rice, silk, and tea producers. Silk and tea, especially, were greatly prized by the rest of the world.

The Southern Sung printed paper money and invented the world's earliest calculator—the abacus. Cities mushroomed in size. Hangchou alone had a population of two million. For the first time in history, the main source of government income shifted from the land to the cities. There was more money to be made taxing silk, tea, pottery, and other trading goods than there was from taxing grain.

This elegant piece of carved, glazed porcelain stoneware was produced by Sung potters.

THE ARTS

Sung potters produced elegant porcelain forms in lovely shades of green, blue, gray, and ivory for export to the West. The secret of making "chinaware" remained with the Chinese until the eighteenth century, when German potters finally figured it out.

As the population in the countryside grew, huge numbers of workers joined the shopkeepers, merchants, and artisans who jammed the cities. The focus of Chinese life, like the tax base, shifted from the countryside to the towns and cities. New, popular art forms developed alongside the traditional arts of the rich. Storytellers wandered the streets charming audiences with yarns, jokes, and folktales. These stories, written down, formed the basis of the Chinese novel and drama.

Paintings by Sung artists showed scenes such as this one, with towering mountains and great rivers, and tiny human figures, houses, or ships at the bottom of the pictures.

Painting, an art form of the wealthy, reached high levels under the Sung. Artists were more interested in nature than in the Buddhist subjects of earlier dynasties. Sung artists painted Taoist themes—serene landscapes that suggested the ideal world of nature. In this world, people were insignificant. Artists painted pictures that showed towering mountains or great rivers, with tiny human figures or houses at the the bottom—a sign that people were inferior to nature. The approach of Chinese painters was very different from most Western artists, who often showed human beings at the center of nature, if they painted nature subjects at all. Chinese artists of that time also were not as interested in color as they were in capturing the spirit of what they were painting. Many pictures from the Sung time are monochromes. That is, they use only one color in several shades.

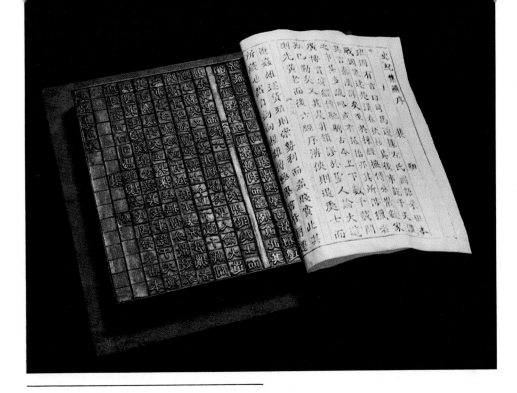

The Chinese invented movable type in 1045.

The Chinese, who taught the world how to make paper, invented printing with movable type in 1045—four hundred years before Gutenberg in the West. Books could be made faster and more cheaply than ever before, which led to a growth in private schools. Increasing numbers of Chinese had access to education. Still, the mandarin class was only a small fraction of China's total population.

SOCIETY

Despite its many achievements, Sung society had its darker side. Poverty spread through the countryside to the towns and cities, where masses of beggars roamed the streets. Never before had China seen so many urban poor. The Sung government put some money aside for food, medicine, and housing for the poor. But most of it ended up in the mandarins' pockets.

The position of women in Chinese life sank to a new low during Sung times. Confucius taught that women were inferior to men, and the Chinese had believed this for centuries. But in earlier days, at least, women workers were vital in keeping the farms going, and everybody knew it. Women's role was not so clear-cut or important in the mass movement to the cities. Among the Sung mandarins, women became little more than playthings or signs of wealth.

The upper classes started to bind their little girls' feet, so that they grew to only half the normal length, with the toes turned under like a hoof. The fact that they could hardly walk made mandarin women seem even more like dolls. In time, the painful practice of foot binding spread throughout China. Until the twentieth century, the "lily foot" was one mark of beauty in a Chinese woman. A girl with normal feet was considered a freak.

At the end of the 1200s, the Sung went the way of earlier ruling families. Yet another barbarian attacked from the north and started his own dynasty. Kublai Khan was no ordinary conqueror, however. He was a prince of a nomad tribe that had subdued most of Asia and terrified Europe before overrunning China.

Chapter 8

THE YUAN
(MONGOL) DYNASTY

When Kublai Khan thundered through the Central Kingdom, he brought China into the vast Mongol Empire, which also included Russia and Persia.

The Mongols were the fiercest fighters the world had ever seen. Mongol children learned to ride horses and fight as soon as they could walk. Women, children, and herds of livestock traveled wherever the troops went, and the Mongols carried with them everything they needed. If they ran out of food in the lands they conquered, it was said they could live on mares' milk alone.

The Chinese have a saying: "A land can be conquered on horseback. But it cannot be ruled that way." The Mongols soon felt the truth of this saying. They knew nothing of farming, or, for that matter, of cities. The dynasty Kublai Khan founded, the Yuan (1280-1368), had to rely on foreigners to run the Chinese government. They let the mandarins continue in lower positions. But the Yuan brought in educated barbarians from other parts of the Mongol Empire to fill high government posts.

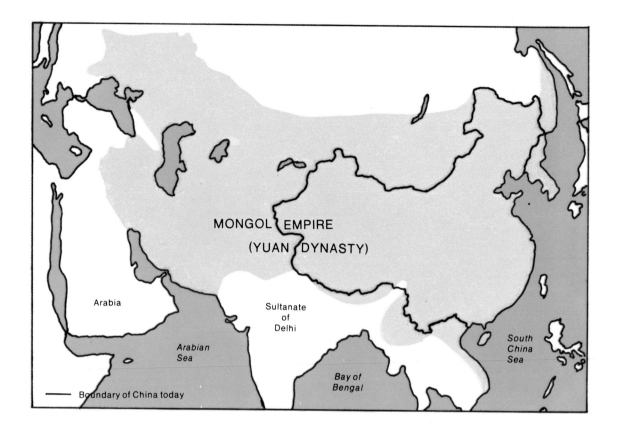

The native Chinese hated these rulers, who were mostly from central Asia. They also hated the measures taken to keep them from rebelling. Native Chinese were not allowed to meet, travel at night, or to make or keep weapons. Even vegetable knives and meat choppers were forbidden.

The Chinese people did not absorb the Mongols into their way of life, as they had other barbarian conquerors. Nor did the Yuan ever really try to become Chinese.

Kublai Khan ruled an empire that spread across Asia into Europe. He was the last of the great Mongol princes. The khan had a wide range of interests, from geography and astronomy to religion. Under Kublai, "square writing" was developed. The new alphabet could be used for any language in the empire.

Kublai Khan (left) the last of the great Mongol princes, founded the Yuan dynasty in 1280.

MARCO POLO

Marco Polo, his father, and his uncle were Italian traders and travelers. They set out from Venice, Italy in 1271. Their destination was China. The trip took more than three years. In China, the Polos learned the Mongol language and the customs of the Yuan dynasty.

They went to work for the Mongol government. They served Kublai Khan for seventeen years and became very wealthy. The khan was reluctant to let them return to Venice, but he finally granted permission. The Polos reached home in 1295.

Venice was at war with Genoa, and Marco was asked to command a Venetian warship. He was captured by the Genoese and spent three years in prison. During that time, he wrote a book about his experiences in China.

For centuries, the Chinese had been fairly well informed about the West. Chang Ch'ien had "discovered" Europe before the birth of Christ. But Marco's report was the first to provide Europe with a thorough description of the East. Many who read it refused to believe that Marco had told the truth. They thought his descriptions of China and the Chinese were fairy tales. But Marco knew otherwise. On his deathbed he insisted he hadn't told half of what he had seen.

Two hundred years later, Christopher Columbus read Marco Polo's book and sailed west across the Atlantic Ocean to find India and China. Instead he accidentally discovered America.

A Yuan dynasty silk painting of a Mongol circus

Throughout the Mongol Empire, it was the custom to seize talented local craft workers and bring them to labor in the capital cities. Under the Yuan dynasty, the high-quality pottery of the Sung period was preserved. Fine cottons were woven, as well as silk. The khan built a capital for his empire at Peking. It was as beautiful and impressive as any Chinese capital before it— complete with palaces, gardens, and man-made lakes. Trade continued to expand, both by land and by sea. The use of paper money in China grew. Chinese ideas and inventions spread rapidly to the rest of the world in the thirteenth and fourteenth centuries.

Arts, crafts, and learning flourished in China under Kublai Khan's rule. But from the beginning, the khan was challenged by his brother, who won the support of the Russian Mongols, known as the Golden Horde. At the end of the thirteenth century, when the Golden Horde became Muslims, relations worsened between Kublai Khan's descendants and the rest of the Mongol Empire.

This Yuan dynasty stoneware bowl was covered with white slip and decorated in colored enamels.

Mongols outside China resented Peking's control. They thought the settled life their kinsmen were leading in China was a disgrace. The Mongol Empire broke up about the same time that the Yuan dynasty lost control in China.

The Yuan rulers who came after Kublai Khan grew weak and corrupt. By the middle of the fourteenth century, the Mongols in China had lost their fighting skills. Most had been born south of the Great Wall and knew little of their ancestors' warlike way of life. Mongol nobles had seized so much land from the peasants that one sixth of the Chinese population was starving.

Secret societies rose up all over China. They began to organize the peasants, who were no longer afraid of their Mongol masters. A Buddhist monk named Chu Yuan-chang led a band of rebels that captured Nanking in 1356. By 1368 he had chased the Yuan from Peking and declared himself the first emperor of the Ming dynasty.

The Imperial Palace, Peking

Chapter 9

THE MING DYNASTY

After almost a century of Mongol rule, the native Chinese were eager to get back to normal. The Ming (1368-1644) restored the study of the *Confucian Classics* and the system of government by mandarins. They tried to get rid of barbarian influences in China and even went so far as to ban foreign styles of dress.

The mandarins' first and most important job was to get the farms working again so that China could feed its hungry masses. There was other work to be done, too. Under the Yuan, the Great Wall had deteriorated. The Ming repaired it and in some spots rebuilt it, along with other defenses against the nomads from the north. Those sections of the Great Wall that stand today date from the Ming period.

The first Ming capital was at Nanking. But Emperor Yung Lo moved his headquarters north to Peking. Within the walls built by Kublai Khan, Yung erected the Imperial City. And inside these walls he built the Forbidden City, a fabulous home for the royal family. Peking became more magnificent than even Kublai Khan had imagined.

Chinese emperors built fabulous, ornate palaces, temples, and other buildings in their capital city of Peking. Among them are the Temple of Heaven (below left), with its beautifully decorated ceiling (above), where the emperors went to pray for a good harvest. The Wall of the Nine Dragons (below) guards a Forbidden City temple from evil spirits.

Above: Statues adorn the roof of the Hall of Supreme Harmony in the courtyard of the Forbidden City. Right: This magnificent bronze lion is one of a pair that guards the entrance to the Forbidden City. Below: A close-up view of the wall ornamentation on one of the buildings in the Forbidden City.

平家情盡在胡笳曲

This Ming dynasty silk painting is one of a series called Eighteen Songs of a Nomad Flute.

Yung Lo dreamed of collecting all of China's wisdom in one great encyclopedia. He put two thousand scholars to work on the project, which filled 11,095 volumes when it was finally finished. A medical encyclopedia produced at the same time described a way of giving shots to prevent a disease called smallpox. The Chinese knew about vaccination some seven hundred years before it was practiced in the West.

Some of the greatest Chinese novels were written under the Ming. Drama, too, flowered. Under the Ming, plays were performed with very little scenery, but elegant costumes. The parts were sung to music performed by a small orchestra. White patches on the villain's face showed craftiness, while lovable characters wore pink makeup. Actors dressed in black were considered to be invisible. Ming potters discovered how to put two and even three colors in their designs. "Chinaware" continued to be highly prized throughout the world.

Cottage beside
the Wu-t'ung Tree,
*a Ming dynasty
painting done
in ink and light
colors on paper*

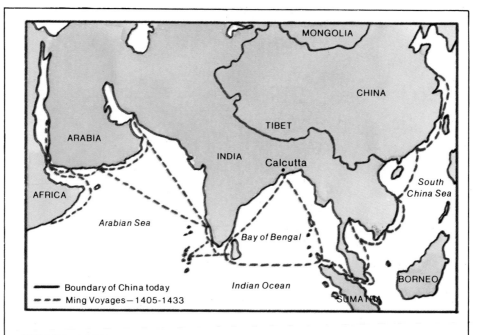

MING VOYAGES

Though shipbuilding made great advances under the Sung, China was never much of a seagoing nation until the Ming took over. Under Emperor Yung Lo, China built a fleet of sixty-two armed ships and practically overnight became an important naval power. In 1405, Admiral Cheng-Ho led an expedition of 28,000 men on the first of seven major voyages. They sailed south and west to Indonesia, Malaya, India, and as far as Africa and the Persian Gulf. The fleets returned to China with all sorts of tribute that never before had been seen, including ostriches, zebras, and giraffes.

These remarkable voyages ended in the 1430s, almost as suddenly as they had begun. After the death of Emperor Yung Lo, Chinese naval expansion stopped.

Under Emperor Yung Lo, the Central Kingdom reached the height of its sea power. Great naval fleets sailed to India, Arabia, and the east coast of Africa.

The Ming were more interested in winning tribute from the countries they sailed to than in fighting with them. The Chinese sent presents of gold and silk to the barbarians, with offers of friendship and trade. The barbarians were supposed to seal the arrangement by sending tribute to the Son of Heaven.

Ming potters produced beautiful porcelain. This lovely bowl is decorated with a red underglaze.

Silk, tea, pottery, and other Chinese goods were in great demand throughout the world. More than thirty countries took up China's offer and sent envoys with presents to Peking. Some of them came from as far away as Italy and Holland.

The Ming did not consider the foreign envoys their equals. To their minds, foreign tribute simply proved that the Chinese emperor really did rule "everything under heaven." The tribute system went back to feudal times, when obedient princes of vassal states sent gifts to the king of Chou as proof of their respect for their lord and master.

Throughout the Ming dynasty, as a reaction against Mongol rule, China was looking backward, trying to restore the glory of the ancient past. The great sea voyages stopped in the 1430s, after Yung Lo's death. Confucian mandarins viewed the rise of commerce and a merchant class as a threat to their power, which was based in the land. Later emperors were more interested in gazing inward than outward toward the rest of the world.

But just the opposite was happening in the West. A great age of sea exploration was beginning. Europe was hungry for new markets. Having sampled Chinese tea, silk, and other goods, the Western nations were determined to trade with China.

This avenue leading to the Ming tombs outside Peking is lined with stone statues of all kinds.

Portuguese ships reached China in 1514. In 1557 the Son of Heaven allowed the Portuguese to set up a trading post on a small southern island called Macao. The Spanish landed in the Philippines in 1565 and started trading with China. Sixty years later, the Dutch arrived, followed by the French and English.

Throughout these years, China's neighbor, Japan, was posing ever more serious problems. For several centuries Japanese pirates had been prowling China's coast. In the late Ming period, the Japanese sailed up the Yangtze to attack Yangchow and Nanking. They later destroyed a Chinese army in Korea.

To these troubles with foreign states was added mounting tension within the country. The Ming dynasty followed the classic pattern of the rise and fall of Chinese ruling families. The first century of Ming rule was stable and prosperous. But by the middle of the period, the court and the mandarins had grown greedy and corrupt. The land was concentrated in the hands of the wealthy few. Ninety percent of the peasants did not own the plots they tilled. Tax laws grew harsher. Some peasants sold their children into slavery or drowned them. Many people killed themselves.

One new twist in the ancient story was that for the first time in Chinese history, city workers revolted. In 1599 the people of Wuchang rose against the tax collector, and the rebellion quickly spread. By the 1630s, most of the northwest was in revolt. Landlords were killed and their holdings divided among the poor. A peasant rebel named Li Tzu-ch'eng united forces from different provinces and in 1644 captured Peking. The Ming emperor hanged himself.

Li Tzu-ch'eng did not live to found a dynasty, however. While rebellion raged within China, a barbarian tribe called the Manchus broke through the Great Wall. Like the Mongols before them, the Manchus set up their own dynasty.

And so the Ming, who had wanted so badly to restore Chinese tradition, were overthrown by traditional means—peasant revolt and barbarian invasion. The new dynasty, the Ch'ing, was to bring China's Imperial Age to a close. The system that had governed the Central Kingdom for more than two thousand years could not survive in the changing world of the nineteenth and twentieth centuries.

This marble boat, built for Empress Tzu-hsi during the Ch'ing dynasty, has a place of honor on Kun-ming Lake at the Summer Palace in Peking.

Chapter 10

THE CH'ING
(MANCHU) DYNASTY

With the arrival of the Manchus, the Chinese empire was once again ruled by foreigners. To remind the native Chinese just who was in power, the Manchus passed a law that all men except monks and priests had to wear their hair in the Manchu style. Instead of the traditional topknot, Chinese men had to shave the front of their heads and wear a pigtail at the back. This was a great insult to the proud Chinese. For forty years after the Manchus took over, resistance continued, especially in the south.

Like the Mongols before them, the Manchus (1644-1911) tried to preserve their own way of life. They kept their own language and customs and did not permit marriage between Manchus and Chinese.

Also like the earlier barbarians, the Manchus found that they lacked the skills to administer the country. They had to rely on the mandarins to keep things running. The Ch'ing continued the old system of selecting government officers on the basis of the civil service tests. But they took steps to keep power in their own hands by a system of checks on the Chinese administrators.

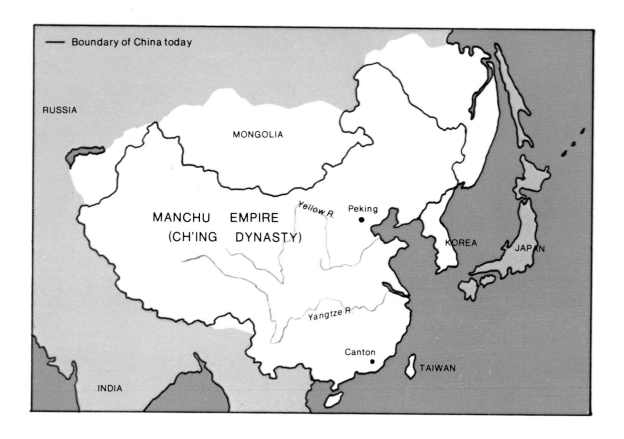

RUSSIA

MONGOLIA

MANCHU EMPIRE
(CH'ING DYNASTY)

Yellow R.

Peking

KOREA

JAPAN

Yangtze R.

Canton

TAIWAN

INDIA

Unlike the Mongols, the Manchus admired the high level of
Chinese art and learning. Ch'ing emperors and their advisers kept
their own culture but also encouraged the development of native
Chinese arts and crafts. They learned the Chinese language and
studied Chinese history and other writings.

EXPANSION AND TRADE

In the first 150 years of the Ch'ing dynasty, the nation benefited
from the capable and extraordinarily long reigns of two men,
K'ang Hsi (1661-1722) and Ch'ien Lung (1736-1795). Both were
men of exceptional ability and dedication. Under them China
enjoyed both peace at home and military success abroad. Once
again the empire reached from the Pacific Ocean to the Pamir
Mountains. Outlying provinces were cleared and settled at an

TEA

Tea was introduced in China during the Han dynasty. First it was used as a medicine, and later as a common drink. The Chinese boiled it with rice, lemon peel, onion, or milk. Later they began to drink it plain. The hilly country south of the Yangtze River is well suited for growing tea, and Chinese tea became a valuable trade item. Tea drinking spread to England and its colonies in the late 1600s, and by the end of the eighteenth century, tea had become China's chief export.

*This exquisite decorative piece was made during the Ch'ing dynasty.
The gilt bronze container is decorated with peonies on enamel, and
the flowers are fashioned of jade, coral, quartz, amber, and ivory.*

A Ch'ing dynasty bowl of lacquer on pewter, inlaid with mother-of-pearl

astonishing pace. Under the Ch'ing, China's working farmland increased by a third. The population was 200 million in 1700 — and that number doubled by 1850.

In the early days of the Ch'ing, traders from Asia and Europe were allowed to do business all along the coast. The West was hungry for Chinese silk, pottery, tea, and other goods. But China was not much interested in anything the barbarians had to offer — except silver. In 1757 the Chinese government confined all foreign trading to one city — Canton. This restriction, and others, did not please the Europeans.

In 1793 England sent its first formal ambassador to the Chinese court. Lord Macartney caused a sensation when he refused to throw himself face down before the Son of Heaven, as was the Chinese custom. This barbarian had come to China to ask the emperor to permit free trade between their nations. The emperor sent back a haughty reply to the king of England. China, he said, "possesses all things in prolific abundance" and had no need for barbarian goods.

China enjoyed a favorable balance of trade until the early 1800s. That is, it sold more goods to other countries than it bought. But growing use of a drug called opium changed the picture dramatically.

THE OPIUM WAR

First the Portuguese and then the British began buying opium in India and selling it in China. In the 1700s, growing numbers of Chinese became addicted to smoking the drug. The Ch'ing tried to stamp out the trade, but their laws were not obeyed. Officials took bribes and traders continued to smuggle the drug ashore. Imported opium rose from two hundred chests a year in 1729 to nineteen thousand chests in 1831. By 1838, thirty thousand chests a year were shipped from India to China.

The government was alarmed. In 1839, Chinese troops surrounded Canton and destroyed $11 million worth of British opium chests. The action led to the Opium War—three years of off-and-on fighting in which British troops overwhelmed Chinese forces.

Under the 1842 Treaty of Nanking, China opened five ports to foreign traders and ceded to Great Britain the island of Hong Kong. The Ch'ing had to pay Britain $21 million in damages. And they even had to agree that the European barbarians would not be subject to Chinese law.

There was not a word about opium in the Treaty of Nanking. After 1852, trade in the drug rose more sharply than ever. So did Chinese imports of other foreign goods, especially textiles. China's balance of trade shifted. Instead of taking in silver, the Central Kingdom was paying it out at a rapid rate. As usual, the burden fell on the peasants. And as usual, the peasants finally rose against the government.

THE TAIPING REBELLION

Several revolts broke out in the decades after China's humiliation by the British. The most serious of these was the Taiping Rebellion, one of the most violent and destructive civil wars in history. Estimates of the number of dead run as high as twenty million.

China, of course, had seen many rebellions in its long history. But there was something different about the Taiping. They weren't just after the overthrow of the Manchus. They wanted to destroy traditional Chinese society.

Like other rebels, the Taiping advocated land reform. They felt that each peasant had a right to own enough land to support an ordinary standard of living. But the Taiping went much further. They put forth the shocking idea that women were equal to men. Women served as soldiers and officers in the rebel army. They also held posts in the government. The Taiping seized wealth from the rich and gave it to the poor. Foot binding, slavery, gambling, drinking, and opium smoking were outlawed.

The Taiping Rebellion was also a religious movement. Its leader, Hung Hsiu-ch'uan, preached a sort of Chinese Christianity. Many of his ideas came from part of a Christian gospel that was translated by a Protestant missionary in Canton. Hung urged his followers to obey the Ten Commandments. He taught that Jesus was the Son of God, sent to earth to redeem sinners.

European missionaries made much of the fact that Hung Hsiu-ch'uan called himself the "younger brother of Jesus." But the Taiping leader never claimed he was divine. "Younger brother" was simply a term denoting a believer. The Taiping word for European Christians, for example, was "foreign younger brothers."

The most the Taiping claimed for their leader was that he was a great prophet, inspired directly by God. In fact, Hung converted millions more to his form of Christianity than any European missionary ever had.

By 1853, the Taiping had fought their way from southeast China to Nanking and made the city their capital. The rebels held on for more than ten years, thanks partly to other revolts in different parts of China that kept the emperor busy. But the Taiping posed too great a threat to the ruling classes. Wealthy landlords and government officials threw their weight behind the Ch'ing dynasty. With help from the West, they raised huge, well-trained armies and equipped them with modern weapons. Finally, in 1864, the rebel capital at Nanking fell to imperial forces. The first and only Taiping ruler killed himself.

UNEQUAL TREATIES

Revolts continued in other parts of the empire for more than a decade. Finally, in the late 1870s, the Ch'ing snuffed out the last of them. But though the fighting was over, the Chinese people continued to smolder against their Manchu masters.

While rebellion raged at home, the Manchus also faced mounting pressure from Europe. The Treaty of Nanking was the first in a long series of "Unequal Treaties" with Western powers that China was forced to sign in the 1840s, 1850s, and 1860s. China lost the right to fix its own tariffs—the taxes charged on foreign goods. After the 1840s, the Manchus could not raise or lower tariffs without permission from the Western powers. China had no control over the many foreigners who swarmed into the trading ports. The Unequal Treaties also provided that any privileges China granted to one Western nation had to be granted to all.

When the Chinese balked at the many restrictions on their rights, war broke out. In 1860 a combined force of French and British troops chased the imperial court from Peking and destroyed the Summer Palace. Eleven more ports were opened to Westerners. A customs service was put under European control. Opium was legalized, and foreign envoys were permitted to live in Peking for the first time in Chinese history. In addition, China sent ambassadors to Western capitals.

The Westerners were not the only barbarians who plagued

During the Ch'ing dynasty, petty criminals were chained together and put on public display so all who saw them would know of the crimes they had committed. This picture was taken in 1895 in Honan Province.

China in the late nineteenth century. After twenty years of rivalry in Korea, Japan and China went to war in 1894. Tough, modern Japanese troops were quick to win, and the war ended with the Treaty of Shimonoseki in 1895. China was forced to recognize the independence of Korea. Taiwan, the Pescadores, and part of Manchuria were turned over to Japan. Finally, the Chinese agreed to pay Japan 200 million ounces (56.7 billion grams) of silver for war damages.

Clearly, the Central Kingdom was crumbling. By the late nineteenth century, France, Britain, Germany, Russia, and Japan all rushed in with knives sharpened for a piece of the Chinese pie. Britain carved its "sphere of influence" in the Yangtze Valley. A sphere of influence was an area of China where a Western power could build railways, naval bases, commercial ports, or whatever else it wanted without competition from other powers or interference from the Chinese government. Manchuria and Mongolia went to Russia; Japan took Fukien Province; Germany's sphere was Shantung Province; and the French claimed southern Kwangtung Province.

*This Robe of State, for summertime wear, was made for
a boy emperor, probably Tzu-hsi's son, T'ung-chih.*

America, busy with developing its own western frontiers, was late in entering the race for spheres of influence in China. The United States adopted an Open Door policy. It called on the other great powers to support "equal trading opportunity" in China and to stop seeking special privileges. America claimed it was trying to protect what remained of Chinese independence. But no one bothered to ask the Chinese if they wanted their door open or closed. To many Chinese, the Open Door policy was America's way of saying "leave some for us."

THE EMPRESS DOWAGER

The person who ruled China during these tremendous changes was Tzu-hsi, the "empress dowager." Her baby son inherited the throne in 1861, when she was twenty-five. She became a regent — someone who rules when the emperor is too young or cannot govern for some other reason. Tzu-hsi stayed in power for almost fifty years — until her death in 1908.

The Empress Dowager Tzu-hsi ruled China from 1861 until her death in 1908.

Tzu-hsi's main goal was to keep the Ch'ing dynasty in power, with herself as its head. By the time she took over, the dynasty was in decline. Mandarins robbed the peasants of their land, kept increasing the tax rates, and pocketed huge amounts of money instead of sending it to the capital. The peasants started to form secret anti-Manchu societies. Their traditional hatred of the Ch'ing was fueled by their resentment of rising foreign influence in China. The generals and viceroys sent to put down armed rebellion became greedy for power. And the barbarians, both European and Japanese, were breaking the doors down.

There is no doubt that the empress dowager was a capable and intelligent person. But she was not in touch with what was really happening in China and knew even less about the outside world. Tzu-hsi was conservative by nature, and little inclined to look for answers to the new problems facing China in the twentieth century. She clung blindly to traditional customs and beliefs — which, after all, had worked pretty well, at least for the ruling classes, for two thousand years.

The pictures on these pages were taken in China about 1870. The city scene is probably Shanghai. Note the Manchu hair style, which all men except monks and priests were forced to wear during the Ch'ing dynasty.

After fifty-five days of hiding in the British Embassy, these Europeans were liberated by an international army that had succeeded in crushing the Boxer Rebellion.

Tzu-hsi did little to relieve the underlying causes of China's trouble. Instead, she fought her personal struggle for power by pitting the groups that threatened her against each other. The Boxer Rebellion was a case in point.

THE BOXER REBELLION

The Boxers were members of a secret society dedicated to getting rid of all foreign influence in China. Also known as the "Society of Harmonious Fists," the group took its name from a boxing ritual practiced by its members. Bands of Boxers attacked foreigners in many parts of the country, especially the north. In June of 1900 Boxer armies, with help from Tzu-hsi's troops, forced one thousand Westerners and three thousand Chinese Christians to hole up in Peking's Legation Quarter for fifty-five days.

By fanning the Boxers' hatred of foreigners, Tzu-hsi kept the rebels from turning against her regime. If the Boxers succeeded in driving the Europeans from China, so much the better for Tzu-hsi.

The Boxer Rebellion proved disastrous, however. Half a dozen Western nations and Japan combined their forces to defeat the rebels. China was forced to pay several hundred million dollars to the West, and the country went deeply into debt. In addition, foreign powers won permanent bases for their troops in Peking.

By the turn of the century, the need for at least some reforms was clear even to the Manchus. Tzu-hsi started to modernize the army. She also permitted some light industry, such as textiles, paper, and shipping, to develop. Heavy industry remained in the hands of foreigners.

The empress faced growing pressure from groups at court to accept and learn from the ways of the West. These groups included a new class of businessmen and traders that emerged in the late nineteenth century. Many scholars, landowners, and other members of the ruling class also saw in Japan's example what could be achieved by modernizing. In 1890 Japan changed to a parliamentary government, without cutting the emperor's power. Japan's military victories against China—and, even more important, in a 1904 war against Russia, a European nation— impressed the Chinese ruling class.

But, to the end, Tzu-hsi hung on to the old ways and remained suspicious of any changes. Even she could see the advantages of Western military methods. But in 1898, when her nephew, the emperor, tried to make changes in education, farming, trade, government, and other areas of Chinese life, Tzu-hsi clapped him into prison.

Over the next decade, the empress dowager slowly began to agree to certain reforms. In 1908 she promised that China would have a constitution and a parliament within nine years. But reforms were too few and came too late. Tzu-hsi died in 1908, and three years later the Central Kingdom became the Republic of China.

This statue of Sun Yat-sen, the first president of the Republic of China, is in Nanking.

Chapter 11

THE REPUBLIC OF CHINA

SUN YAT-SEN

Many rebel groups were at work in the empire in the closing days of the Ch'ing. In 1905, Sun Yat-sen, son of a Canton farmer, united these groups to form the Revolutionary League. Its program consisted of the Three People's Principles: Nationalism, Democracy, and the People's Livelihood.

Nationalism meant that China should be free to run its own affairs without interference from foreigners. Democracy meant rule by a parliament and a constitution—not by a dynasty that inherited power. The People's Livelihood meant that the land and other resources of China should be managed for the benefit of the masses of people, not just to fatten the ruling class.

Sun Yat-sen, the founder of the Revolutionary League, was a Christian. As a young man he studied in Hawaii and Hong Kong, and traveled to London. In the 1890s he formed a secret anti-Manchu society. By 1895 there was a price on his head in China, and he had to leave the country. He traveled to Japan, America, and England, trying to raise money and support for his one dream—to see China become a republic.

Sun was in America in December of 1911. When revolution exploded in China on January 1, 1912, he was sworn in as the first president of the Republic of China (1912-1949).

YUAN SHIH-K'AI

The main reason the revolution had succeeded so quickly was
that Yuan Shih-k'ai, the general of the imperial army, went over
to the rebels. Yuan's troops were well trained, well equipped, and
well paid. They were very loyal to their general. Yuan probably
could have held off the rebel forces for some time, if not beaten
them. But he knew the Manchus' days were numbered. And he
had his own dreams of power.

Yuan agreed to support the new republic—if he could be its
chief. After only forty-three days in office, Sun Yat-sen resigned to
save the constitution. But Yuan's idea of a constitution was a far
cry from Sun's Three People's Principles. The new document
excluded most Chinese from voting. It said nothing about land
reform or equality between men and women. In 1914 Yuan had
himself proclaimed President for Life and changed the
constitution so that the post would pass to his son. Yuan turned
out to be nothing but another warlord who wanted to set up his
own dynasty.

WORLD WAR I

World War I brought Japanese troops to Chinese soil once
again. This time, the Japanese were allies of Great Britain, France,
Italy, and other Western powers at war with Germany. In 1915
Japan secretly made a series of demands on Yuan's government
for special privileges in China. Among other things, Japan wanted
to oversee the workings of the Chinese government and police
force. In effect, the Twenty-one Demands would have made China
a Japanese protectorate. Yuan went public with the Twenty-one

Demands, hoping for help from the West. Japan withdrew its most extreme demands, but China was forced to sign a treaty granting the rest of them.

Yuan Shih-k'ai died in 1916, and warlords took over whole provinces. They were powerless against the Japanese, who, with "permission" from the Western allies, took control over the former German concessions in the Shantung peninsula at the end of World War I.

The revolution had been double-crossed. Sun fell back and reorganized the Revolutionary League into the Kuomintang, or National People's Party. But poverty and disunity plagued China for another decade as the warlords dominated the country.

COMMUNISM, CHOU EN-LAI, AND CHIANG KAI-SHEK

In the late teens and early twenties, many reform-minded Chinese turned to the teachings of Marx, Lenin, and other European Communists for answers to China's problems. They formed the Chinese Communist Party in 1921. Communist ideas spread rapidly, especially among the ever-growing numbers of city workers in China.

In 1923 the Kuomintang began to admit Communists as members. Together, Nationalists and Communists set up a revolutionary government in Canton. They also founded a military academy to train an army to send against the warlords. A Communist, Chou En-lai, was the political director of Whampoa Military Academy. Advisers and equipment came from the Soviet Union. The dean of Whampoa Military Academy was Chiang Kai-shek, who became the leader of the Kuomintang after Sun's death in 1925.

Chiang was not a Communist. The son of a wealthy landowner, he had strong anti-Manchu beliefs and put them into practice in his military career. He met Sun Yat-sen about 1920 and became his military adviser.

Chiang commanded the Northern Expedition, which set out from Canton in 1926 against the northern warlords. He had a lot of help from the Communists. One of the Kuomintang's important goals was to capture Shanghai, China's richest city. While Chiang's army was fighting its way north, Shanghai Communists, led by Chou En-lai, called a general strike in the city. Workers overthrew the local warlords, seized the police station and other key posts, and set up a city government. By the time Chiang arrived, the battle had been won.

The Shanghai strike proved how powerful the Communists had become. But Chiang did not really believe in the Three People's Principles. He was in favor of Nationalism and the modernization of the Chinese state. But he soon proved that he was not really interested in Democracy or the People's Livelihood. Chiang had powerful business interests to protect, and he won the support of both Chinese and foreigners who were threatened by the rise of communism in China.

Two weeks after the warlords disappeared from Shanghai, Chiang turned on the Communists. He shot down thousands in the streets of Shanghai. Communists in other cities and in the countryside also were rooted out and killed.

Chiang set up a government in Nanking in 1927. He made membership in the Chinese Communist Party a crime punishable by death. By April, Communist numbers had dropped from fifty thousand to about ten thousand. Chiang even turned against non-Communists in the Kuomintang who supported the Three

Chiang Kai-shek, who gained control of the Nationalist Party after the death of Sun Yat-sen in 1925, turned against the Communists in 1927.

COMMUNISM

Karl Marx (1818-1883) is often called the father of the Communist movement. He was a German philosopher, social scientist, and revolutionary. With the help of Friedrich Engels (1820-1895), another leading Communist thinker, Marx wrote the *Communist Manifesto* (1848), *Das Kapital* (1867), and many political articles that set forth Communist views.

Marx saw history as one long struggle between the workers and the ruling classes who owned the land, factories, and other means of production. As long as these resources were privately owned, Marx wrote, the working classes were bound to suffer. Farm and factory profits would build up in the hands of the owners, and workers would have a smaller and smaller share in the rewards of their labor.

Marx thought the free-enterprise system, or capitalism, was doomed. He admitted that it had produced great wealth in the highly industrialized West. But a system that exploits the working classes is bound to collapse, said Marx. Capitalism had already led to widespread misery. When things got bad enough, the workers would revolt. They would seize the land, the factories, and other means of production and run them for the common good. Everyone would share equally in profits. There would be no more conflicts between owners and workers, rich and poor. Everyone would belong to the same class. The march of history, said Marx, was toward public ownership of a community's resources.

Marx expected that communism would first take hold in a highly industrialized country, such as England or Germany. In fact, the first successful Communist revolution occurred in Russia, a country that was beginning to industrialize but was still mainly rural. V.I. Lenin (1870-1924) and other revolutionaries drew on Marx and Engels and added their own ideas in founding the Union of Soviet Socialist Republics in 1917. The writings of Lenin and Marx inspired Mao Tse-tung, Chou En-lai, and other founders of the Chinese Communist Party.

People's Principles. Sun Yat-sen's widow, and others who shared her beliefs, fled the country.

Once again the revolution had been double-crossed. The Kuomintang was a National People's Party in name only. In 1931 Japan invaded Manchuria, where much of China's heavy industry had been developed by the Russians and Japanese. Instead of fighting the Japanese, the Nationalists concentrated on rooting out the Communists, who had taken to the mountains in Kiangsi and Hunan. There the party began to organize the peasants. At the end of 1931, the Communists proclaimed a Chinese Soviet Republic in Kiangsi.

By 1933 Communist numbers had reached 300,000. In areas governed by the Chinese Soviet Republic, with Mao Tse-tung as chairman, landlords and officials were driven out or killed. Their lands were given to the peasants, who elected their own councils, or *soviets*. Opium smoking and gambling were outlawed, as were slavery, arranged marriages, and begging. Women gained equal rights with men.

Chiang threw almost everything he had into a series of "campaigns to stamp out the bandits." As many as a million peasants may have died in the crossfire. The last and most serious campaign pitched a Nationalist army of almost half a million troops against a hundred thousand Red Army rifles.

MAO TSE-TUNG

In the autumn of 1934, the Communists were holed up and fighting for their lives in South Kiangsi, blockaded in the west and south by Nationalist forces. On October 16, the Red Army broke through the blockade and began one of the most incredible feats

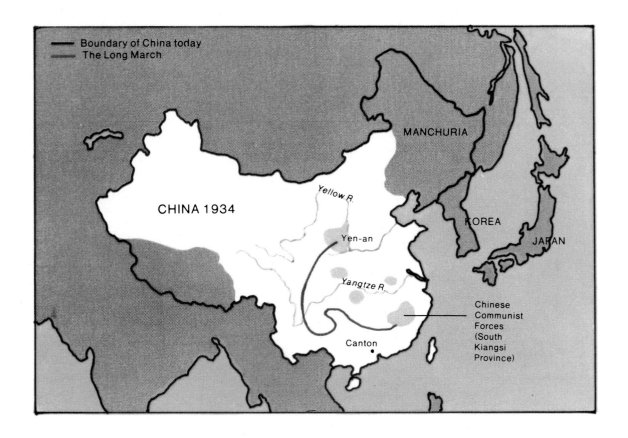

Boundary of China today
The Long March

MANCHURIA

CHINA 1934

Yellow R.

Yen-an

KOREA

JAPAN

Yangtze R.

Chinese
Communist
Forces
(South
Kiangsi
Province)

Canton

of Chinese history. Mao Tse-tung led more than a hundred thousand men, women, and children on the "Long March." They traveled—on foot—more than 6,000 miles (9,700 kilometers) across mountains, rivers, and swamps, through some of the most difficult terrain in China. Only about twenty thousand survived the yearlong journey to Shensi Province in the north. There a soviet government similar to Hunan's had been established. But along the way, the "Poor People's Army" won the support of millions of peasants.

In 1935 Mao issued a call to all the Chinese people to unite against the Japanese. "Chinese do not fight Chinese," he said. By December of 1936, anti-Japanese feelings were so strong that Chiang Kai-shek's own generals kidnapped him and forced him to join a United Front with the Communists against the Japanese.

In 1937, Japanese invading forces (above) overran Shanghai and Nanking.

It was a losing battle. In 1937 Japan launched a massive
invasion of China. By the end of the year, Shanghai and the
capital, Nanking, fell to the Japanese. A year later they controlled
most of eastern China. After World War II broke out in 1939,
Japan was no longer in a position to extend its hold on China.
Chiang kept a number of Japanese divisions pinned down, and the
war front stabilized. In 1941, the year America entered World
War II, Chiang resumed his attacks on the Communists.

Japan surrendered to the Allied forces in August of 1945, after
America dropped the first atomic bombs on Hiroshima and

This home in pre-1948 China was built into a hillside.

Nagasaki. The war between the Nationalists and Communists dragged on for another four years. Although Chiang had begun with a four-to-one edge in troops and weapons, and had received economic and military aid from the United States, he lacked the support of the vast majority of China's population. There were many reasons for this, but foremost among them were his failure to fight the Japanese and the widespread corruption of his government and generals. Many members of his government made fortunes in the war while millions of Chinese citizens starved and suffered.

Mao Tse-tung, chairman of the Chinese Communist Party from 1935 until his death in 1976

MAO TSE-TUNG

Mao Tse-tung, a brillant general and political thinker, helped found the Chinese Communist Party and the People's Republic of China. He was born to a middle-class peasant family in Hunan Province on December 26, 1893. By the time he died, just short of his eighty-third birthday, he had changed the course of history.

China was still ruled by the Empress Dowager Tzu-hsi when Mao was a schoolboy. As the family's oldest son, Mao learned to read and write classical Chinese at the village school. In 1911, the year the Manchu dynasty fell, Mao spent six months in the revolutionary army. Then he entered the first Teacher's Training School at Ch'angsha.

Mao was deeply concerned about China's future and was disappointed with the failure of the new republic to deal with the country's pressing problems. He founded a revolutionary magazine and joined radical student groups. After graduation in 1918, he worked as a library assistant at Peking University. Mao read Marx's *Communist Manifesto* early in 1920. By the fall of that year, he was back in Hunan teaching Marxism.

Mao played a major role in organizing the Chinese Communist Party in 1921. But he did not become its undisputed leader for many years. Within the Chinese Communist Party there were several important men who accepted Marx's teaching that a successful Communist revolution had to be based on the support of urban industrial workers. Mao disagreed very strongly with these men. He believed that Chinese communism's greatest hope and strength lay in the hundreds of millions of peasants. It took him nearly fifteen years to convince his fellow Communists of this truth. Before he did, however, many people had to fight and die in China's cities.

There also were wars to be fought. The first was against Chiang Kai-shek and his Nationalist forces, who turned on the Communists in 1927. Next came the Japanese, who took over large sections of China before and during World War II. Mao also fought many political battles. Not until 1935 was he elected chairman of the Chinese Communist Party. He held the post until his death in 1976.

Mao led the Chinese Communists to victory over the Nationalists and founded the People's Republic of China in 1949. He was a driving force in transforming China from a weak, backward nation to a major power. Under him, China's land and other resources were divided more equally than ever before. The revolution touched every aspect of Chinese life—from the organization of work and family life to education, art, and entertainment. The revolution also cost many Chinese lives. Estimates of the number who died during Mao's rule run into tens of millions.

Entrance building to the Mao Tse-tung Memorial in Peking

THE PEOPLE'S REPUBLIC OF CHINA

The Communists, on the other hand, had won the support of the Chinese people. The force of the peasants, said Mao, was "like the raging winds and driving rain." By the fall of 1949, the storm of revolution had peaked. Nationalist troops deserted to the Communists in large numbers, and Chiang Kai-shek fled to the island of Taiwan, off China's coast. On October 1, 1949, Mao Tse-tung announced the formation of the People's Republic of China. To this day, the Republic of China is confined to the island of Taiwan.

The victory of the Chinese Communists marked a turning point in world history. The ancient system that had ruled China for two thousand years was replaced by a government as different from it as night from day. In thirty years, the People's Republic has become a major world power. Today, Chinese Communists govern one of every five people on earth.

The People's Republic faces the same two problems that toppled the Manchu dynasty: How to feed a rapidly rising population when most of China's land is not suitable for farming, and how to acquire the industry and skills necessary for a nation in the modern world. In grappling with these problems, the Chinese Communists have transformed their society in one of the most amazing social changes the world has ever seen.

MINI-FACTS AT A GLANCE

GENERAL INFORMATION ON PRE-1949 CHINA

Official Name: Republic of China (in mainland China); in 1949, the government of the Republic of China, under Chiang Kai-shek, moved to the island of Taiwan.

Capital: Nanking

Official Language: Mandarin Chinese. Only one written language was used throughout the country. The spoken language, however, was grouped into three main families: Indo-Chinese, Austro-Asiatic, and Altai.

Government: Mainland China was a republic using the same basic system of government that is used today in Taiwan. It is based on the five-power system originated by Dr. Sun Yat-sen, the founder of the Republic of China. Under the president of the republic, who in 1948 was Generalissimo Chiang Kai-shek, there were five *yuan* (branches of government): executive, legislative, judicial, examination, and control. The examination yuan ran the civil service system, which had been in existence for 2,500 years. The control yuan oversaw the conduct of public officeholders and had the power to impeach them. The president served for six years. The president of the executive yuan, whose position was similar to a premier in other democracies, was appointed by the president of the republic with the consent of the legislative yuan. China was divided into 35 provinces and a territory (Tibet), each with its own local government.

Flag: The flag of the republic (also the flag of the Republic of China in Taiwan) was officially adopted in 1928. It is referred to as the White-Sun-in-Blue-Sky-over-Red-Ground flag. A 12-point white sun on a dark blue background sits at the upper left-hand corner of an otherwise plain red flag.

National Song: The words to the national anthem, ''Three People's Principles Song,'' were written by Dr. Sun Yat-sen. The music was written by Cheng Mao-yun.

Religion: Many religions were practiced in mainland China, including ancestor-worship, Confucianism, Taoism, Buddhism, Lamaism, Mohammedanism, and Catholicism. It is difficult to estimate how many people practiced each religion, but the following statistics give an idea of how many people formally affiliated themselves with a religion circa 1946-47. There were 4,620,000 members of the Chinese Buddhist Society, an estimated 50 million Muslims, and 3,279, 813 Catholics.

Money: As a result of wartime conditions, the Chinese currency was very unstable in the 1930s and 1940s. In order to bring order to the situation, the government introduced the gold *yuan* on August 19, 1948, which was supposed to end the inflation that was crippling the economy. There were gold *yuan* notes worth 1, 5, 10, 20, 50, and 100 *yuan*. There were also the *chiao* and the *fen*. Ten *fen* made one *chiao*. Ten *chiao* made one *yuan*. Among the *fen* and *chiao*, there were five denominations: 1 *fen*, 5 *fen*, 1 *chiao*, 2 *chiao*, and 5 *chiao*.

Weights and Measures: The Chinese had their own system of weights and measures different from either the English system or the metric. For example, two *Shih Li* were equal to one kilometer or 0.6214 miles. Two *Shih Chin* were equal to one kilogram or 2.2046 pounds.

Population: 462,798,093, according to a 1947 census. Because of the difficult conditions under which this census was taken, this number should be regarded as an estimate.

Administrative Districts: Although post-World War II China had one fifth of the world's population, the overall population density was low. Generally speaking, the most densely populated areas were where agriculture flourished. This accounts for the fact that the population of desolate Tibet, while a large province, was only one million.

Szechwan	47,437,387
Honan	29,654,095
Taiwan	6,384,019
*Shanghai	4,630,385
*Peking	1,721,546
*Nanking	1,113,972
Tibet	1,000,000

(Population figures as of June, 1948)

*Indicates cities. The rest of the administrative districts are provinces.

GEOGRAPHY

Highest Point: Mount Kunlun in Sinkiang-Tibet-Chinghai, 25,341 ft. (7,724 m)

Coastline: China has two coastlines. In 1948, the length of the continental coastline was 6,897 mi. (11,097 km) and the length of the islandic coastline was 12,862 mi. (20,695 km).

Rivers: The longest river in China is the Yangtze, 3,346 mi. (5,384 km)

Lakes: Lake Kokonor in Chinghai Province is China's largest lake. Its surface area is 1,622 sq. mi. (4,200 km²).

Limestone hills on the Li River near Kuei-lin in southern China

Mountains: China is a mountainous country. It is estimated that regions 3,281 ft. (1,000 m) or more above sea level make up more than 68 percent of the total area of China.

Climate: Because China is very large, its climate ranges from tropical to subarctic. But the difference in latitude is not the only factor influencing climate. There are also two others: altitude and distance from the sea. The city of Shanghai, on the coast, has an average January temperature of 38° F. (3.3° C) and an average July temperature of 80° F. (26.7° C). Urumchi, located in the interior, has an average January temperature of -3° F. (-19.4° C) and a July average of 75° F. (23.9° C). On the whole, China has a greater temperature variance from summer to winter than does the United States, with hotter summers and colder winters.

Rain falls mostly in the summer and much more on the southeast coast than other places. Parts of the interior have too little rain to support crops. There are large regions of deserts and steppes that are very desolate. The chief deserts are the Gobi, the Ordos, the Ningsia, and the Takla Makan. Even in areas that are not deserts, the rainfall is unpredictable. Since the beginning of recorded history, China has been plagued by drought and floods.

Greatest Distances: None recorded because the borders were in dispute immediately following World War II.

Area: It was estimated that the area of China was 3,789,320 sq. mi. (9,814, 338 km²), excluding the exact area measurements of Dairen and Mukden.

NATURE

Trees: There are many kinds of trees in China. In the north, there are oak, maple, linden, birch, Korean pine, walnut, and elm. In the temperate climates, there are ginkgo and metasequoia, both species that are more than 60 million years old. In the southern and southwestern provinces, there are 150 species of evergreen. Bamboo trees are found in large numbers south of the Yangtze. In the area bordering Korea, there are larch, spruce, and fir.

Animals: In the tundra—reindeer, arctic hare, arctic fox, wolf, and lemming. South of the tundra—brown bear, wolf, wolverine, otter, ermine, sable, lynx, elk, forest reindeer, hare, and several kinds of squirrel. In the mountains—takin or goat antelope. In and near Tibet—giant pandas and wild yak.

Birds: In and around Tibet—pheasant, varieties of laughing thrushes. In the tundra—willow grouse, ptarmigan, the gray plover, knot, and several kinds of sandpiper. South of the tundra—black grouse, hazel hen, black woodpecker, Siberian jay, and greater and lesser spotted woodpeckers.

Fish and other water animals: In the Yangtze—the great paddlefish. In east central China—small species of alligator. In western China—giant salamander.

EVERYDAY LIFE

Food: Although food was scarce during World War II, the province of Szechwan was relatively well supplied because the food was grown locally. For example, foods widely grown in the province were rice, wheat, corn, potatoes, turnips, cabbages, pears, peaches, grapes, dates, chestnuts, walnuts, and peanuts. Beef was much cheaper than pork and chickens, while ducks and geese were too expensive for most pocketbooks, unless they were raised at home. Milk was hard to get, but the Chinese are not fond of it. Butter was not a common sight, either. Coffee was very expensive, but the Chinese prefer tea, which was grown in the area in abundance.

It was not unusual for the Szechwanese to eat four meals a day. A common breakfast consisted of bean milk and crullers (doughnutlike cakes). A late meal, after lunch and dinner, often consisted of noodles, dumplings, congee (stewed rice), or sweets. Szechwanese food is famous throughout the world. Most dishes from this southwestern province are spiced with small red chilis, unlike Cantonese food, which is sweeter and more colorful than food from other regions, or food from Shanghai, which is salty.

Homes: Many homes were destroyed by the Japanese during World War II. In some towns—Chungking, for example—buildings of brick and stone were turned to rubble. In their places were erected temporary buildings of mud and bamboo. The roofs were of crude tile or rice straw.

Holidays: (National)
January 1, Formal Founding of the Republic of China (1912)
March 29, Martyr's Day (Youth Day)
August 27, Confucius's Birthday (Teachers' Day)
October 10, National Day
November 12, Dr. Sun Yat-sen's Birthday Anniversary

Culture: The Chinese are great opera lovers. More than 700 years ago—during the Yuan dynasty, when China was ruled by the Mongols—there was a dramatic art form that resembled modern opera. Chinese literature and art are even older. Chinese silk painting is thought to go back to the third century B.C. From the beginning, Chinese painting, calligraphy, and poetry went together, almost as one art form. In traditional Chinese art, poems were written in calligraphy on a landscape. The Chinese had "different" notions about what is art. Traditionally, they did not view their magnificent architecture or porcelain painting as art. These works, they believed, were done by artisans rather than artists, and the Chinese made sharp distinctions between the two.

Sports and Recreation: Athletics in China originally were associated with military training. The earliest forms were boxing, wrestling, and archery. In modern times, the American YMCA influenced the pattern of involvement in sports. The first such institution, set up in 1895 in China, promoted physical education and competitive sports. In the 1920s, foreign influence declined as China became nationalistic. In 1927, provincial and national physical education institutes were established by the Chinese government. The Chinese Communist Party had its own sports program in the 1930s and 1940s.

Communications: At the end of 1948, there were 2,069 news publications registered with the government. Of these, nearly three fourths—1,372—were daily newspapers. The rest were two-day, three-day, and five-day journals; weeklies; semimonthlies; and monthlies. There were 1,899 periodicals, mostly weekly and monthly magazines, registered with the government. There were 412 weekly publications and 981 monthly publications.
In March, 1948, the Central Broadcasting Administration had 42 radio stations under its auspices. Programs were broadcast in various languages. For example, news programs in *kuoyu* or Mandarin (the national spoken language) and in English done in studios in Nanking were rebroadcast by affiliate stations. Some of the programs originated in the United States or the United Kingdom. All CBA stations devoted a considerable amount of time to newscasts done in 18 languages and dialects.

Transportation: China's railroads suffered greatly from wartime destruction. At the end of 1947, 8,497 mi. (13,675 km), less than half of the total railway length in China, was open to traffic. As for water traffic, it is estimated that 9,320 mi. (15,000 km) of waterways were navigable for steamships, and another 14,913 mi. (24,000 km) for junks and sailboats. After World War II, all old shipping routes were restored, with Shanghai as the central port. There was also a program to restore and add to the highway system in the country. Airline traffic saw the most rapid development of all kinds of transportation during and just after World War II because it was the most flexible kind of transportation. In 1948, there were three airlines—the China National Aviation Corporation, the Central Air Transportation Corporation, and the Civil Air Transport.

Schools: Children between the ages of six and twelve attended primary schools. During the 1940s, the Chinese government made a concerted effort to educate its school-age children and eliminate illiteracy. New schools were established in accordance with a five-year plan adopted at the National Conference on People's Education held in March of 1940. The program was extended for five more years beginning in January of 1946. The next level of education fell into one of three categories: ordinary middle schools, vocational schools, and normal schools. Middle schools prepared children for higher education. They offered a six-year program divided into two stages of three years each, called junior and senior middle schools. Vocational schools prepared youngsters for particular trades or technical vocations such as civil engineering, agriculture, or weaving. The so-called normal schools trained teachers. At the close of the war, there were 145 institutions of higher learning. There had been an increase in enrollment and in the number of schools since the beginning of the war with Japan in 1937. This was in spite of the fact that many schools had been hit by the enemy or had to move out of their original campuses, sometimes more than once, in order to avoid being in war zones.

Health: The Chinese suffered from many health problems during the 1940s, mostly due to the effects of the war. Combat injuries, poor nutrition, rapid spread of epidemics, and lack of adequate medical service accounted for a very high mortality rate. At the end of 1946, medical personnel registered with the National Health Administration numbered only 30,343, including 13,447 doctors.

Principal Products:
Agriculture: Soybeans, broad beans, rice, wheat, millet, peanuts, tea, tobacco, and silk
Minerals: Tungsten concentrate, antimony metal, refined tin, and mercury
Chief exports: Oils, tallow, and wax; animals and animal products; yarn, thread, and plaited and knitted goods; textile fibers; beans and peas; and tea

MONGOL LIFE

Food: The Mongols lived on meat, milk, and game. They also ate horse meat and dog meat, and drank mares' milk.

Houses: A nomadic group, the Mongols lived in portable, circular tents supported by wooden rods and covered with felt. They were transported on ox-pulled or camel-drawn wagons.

Mongol Way of Life: The Mongol way of life was rugged, so much so that there was little difference between peace and war. The Mongols lived on horseback because the steppes that they inhabited offered little good grazing. In the summer they migrated north, and in winter they trekked south. They used the same bows and arrows to kill animals or people. When they won a battle, they killed all the men and subjected the women and children to slavery. Mongols measured wealth by the number of silks, furs, and animals a man possessed.

IMPORTANT DATES

400,000 years ago—Peking Man lived

4500-3000 B.C.—Neolithic period

circa 2500 B.C.—China's Golden Age

circa 2000 B.C.—Yü founds the Hsia dynasty

481-221 B.C.—Warring States period

221-206 B.C.—The unification of China under the Ch'in dynasty; Legalism adopted as state philosophy

221-207 B.C.—Emperor Shih Huang-ti builds the Great Wall

202 B.C.-A.D. 22—Confucianism declared the state philosophy under Han dynasty

221-589—Age of Disunity

907-960—Warlords take over

1126—Barbarian Kin armies capture Kaifeng, the Sung capital

1045—Chinese invent movable type

1356—Chu Yuan-chang captures Nanking

1368—Mongol rule overthrown

1514—Portuguese ships reach China

1557—The Portuguese set up a trading post on the island of Macao

1565—The Spanish land in the Philippines and start trading with China

1644—Li Tzu-ch'eng captures Peking

1757—All foreign trade confined to Canton

1793—England sends its first formal ambassador to the Chinese court

1839—Opium War between China and Great Britain

1842—Treaty of Nanking ends Opium War

1851-1864—The Taiping Rebellion

1895—Treaty of Shimonoseki (China recognizes the independence of Korea)

1900-1901—Boxer Rebellion

1904-1905—Russo-Japanese War and partition of Manchuria

1911—Revolution

1912—Sun Yat-sen becomes first president of the Republic of China

1914—Yuan Shih-k'ai has himself proclaimed President for Life

1915—Japan presents its Twenty-one Demands to China

1916—Yuan Shih-k'ai dies; warlords take over in China

1921—Chinese Communist Party founded

1923—The Kuomintang admits Communists to its membership

1925—Nationalist government formed at Canton; Chiang Kai-shek becomes the leader of the Kuomintang

1926—Chiang Kai-shek commands Northern Expedition against the warlords

1927—Chiang Kai-shek sets up Nationalist government at Nanking

1931—Japan invades Manchuria; Communists proclaim the Chinese Soviet Republic of Kiangsi

1932—Manchuria declared independent

1934-1935—Long March north from South Kiangsi to Shensi Province, led by Mao Tse-tung

1936—Chiang Kai-shek kidnapped

1937—Japan invades China

1941—Chinese-Japanese war merges into World War II

1945—Japan surrenders, end of World War II

1948—Fall of Manchuria to the Communists

1949—People's Republic of China proclaimed

IMPORTANT PEOPLE

An Lu-shan (A.D.703-757), leader of a rebellion against the T'ang dynasty

Chang Heng (circa A.D.100), invented the seismograph

Chiang Kai-shek (1887-1975), president of the Republic of China

Chou En-lai (1898-1976), Chinese Communist leader

Chu Hsi (1130-1200), philosopher whose reinterpretation of Confucian teachings was to have great influence on China's official class up to the twentieth century

Chu Yuan-chang (reigned 1368-98), first emperor of the Ming dynasty

Confucius (551-479 B.C.), one of China's greatest teachers, author of a code of behavior that lasted until the twentieth century

Hsuan-tsung (685-762), T'ang emperor whose reign ended with the An Lu-shan rebellion

Hsun-tzu (298-238 B.C.), first scholar-official, based a practical political and social philosophy on adherence to culture, or ceremony and ritual

Huang-ti (reigned 2697-2597 B.C., mythical dates), legendary founder of Chinese civilization

Hung Hsiu-ch'uan (1814-1864), leader of the Taiping Rebellion

Kao-tsung (649-683), emperor and husband of Empress Wu

Kublai Khan (1216-1294), founder of the Mongol dynasty

Lao-tzu (575-485? B.C.), legendary first teacher of Taoism

Li Po (A.D.701-762), poet

Li Shih-min (600-649), first T'ang emperor

Li Tzu-ch'eng (circa 1606-1645), peasant rebel against the Ming dynasty

Mao Tse-tung (1893-1976), leader of the Chinese Communist Party and founder of the People's Republic of China

Mencius (372-289 B.C.), follower of Confucius, taught that people who worked with their heads were superior to those who worked with their hands

Mo-tzu (circa 479-438 B.C.), leader of the Mohists, preached universal love

Shang Yang (circa 400-338 B.C.), important Legalist and chief minister to the king of Ch'in

Shih Huang-ti (259-209 B.C.), first ruler to unify China, builder of Great Wall of China

Sun Yat-sen (1866-1925), founder of the Revolutionary League and founding father of the Republic of China

Tu Fu (712-770), poet

Tzu-hsi, the Empress Dowager (1836-1908), powerful Ch'ing ruler

Wu (624-705), empress of the T'ang dynasty

Yang Ti (reigned 605-618), second Sui emperor, famous for extravagant public works projects

Yü (circa 2000 B.C.), semilegendary founder of the Hsia dynasty

Yuan Shih-k'ai (1859-1916), general of the imperial army during the 1911 revolution and later president of the republic

Yung Lo (1360-1424), third emperor of the Ming dynasty, sponsored a great encyclopedia of 11,095 volumes

DYNASTIES

Hsia	circa 2000 B.C.
Shang	18th century B.C.-12th century B.C.
Chou	about 1122-221 B.C.
Ch'in	221-206 B.C.
Han	202 B.C.-A.D. 221
Age of Disunity	221-589
The Second Empire:	
Sui	589-618
T'ang	618-907
Five Dynasties	907-960
Sung	960-1280
Yuan (Mongol)	1280-1368
Ming	1368-1644
Ch'ing (Manchu)	1644-1911

Birch-tree-lined country road outside Peking

A farmer meditates on a hill near Sian.

INDEX

Page numbers that appear in boldface type indicate illustrations

About the Author

Valjean McLenighan, a graduate of Knox College in Galesburg, Illinois, became interested in writing children's books during her stint as an editor at a large midwestern publishing company. Since that time, many of her children's books have been published.

Though she nearly always has a book project in the works, Valjean finds time for a variety of other interests including the theater, children's television, and travel. She lives on the North Side of Chicago.